Your Design Personality at Home

Unlock the secrets of your interior design style

Michelle Armitage

FRANK
INTERIORS

First published in Great Britain in 2023 by
Light and Frank Publishing
www.lightandfrank.com

ISBN 978-1-916525-00-9

Cover and inside page design by Berenice Howard-Smith,
Hello Lovely

Proofread by Annie Deakins, Proofnow

Image credits on page 215

Contents

Introduction

Have you ever walked into a room and felt immediately uncomfortable, but not known why? Or the opposite; entered a room so beautiful, so perfect, that you have felt instantly boosted, comfortable and 'at home'? Wouldn't you love to know how to avoid the first and create the second? The secrets inside this book will help you find out how.

The amount of advice and choices in the world of Interior Design are phenomenal. It's no wonder it can feel overwhelming. As an interior designer, I find that feeling overwhelmed and having a lack of confidence about design choices are common problems, both for my clients and for many other people I talk to. They ask me for help with ideas and inspiration, but they often need just as much help with sorting through options and making decisions. Getting the process wrong can be costly. We've all bought a sofa that was too big or a lamp that was too small. That rug that looked so lovely in the shop, but, oh the disappointment, when it just doesn't look right upon arrival at home! And, when it comes to buying a new kitchen or bathroom, the wrong choice can feel like a disaster!

Kitchen companies offer free designs and consultations, but they rarely help you think about what kind of cooking you do, how sociable you are, what styles you like and so on. That's not the fault of the kitchen companies. Their job is to give you a quality kitchen to your specification.

This book will help you create a picture of your needs and ideas, so you can walk into the kitchen showroom feeling confident that you know what you want AND how to describe it.

A relaxed and sophisticated lounge design

Navigating overwhelming choices

There are times when choosing interiors can feel too much. The bigger the job, the more decisions you have to make. I get asked all manner of seemingly random questions by my clients such as: What colour should I paint this room? Is magnolia my best bet or should I use bright colours? Should I go for the industrial look, or more boho? How often should I redecorate? These questions reveal so much to me; that people just don't know where to start, and also that they have so little confidence in their design abilities. Many of these clients have a love of interiors magazines, and enjoy following people's ideas on Instagram and Pinterest. Maybe you're the same? But sometimes, it seems to me that the sheer volume of advice and choice out there can suck all the joy from what should be a fun and creative process.

Added to choice overwhelm is the comparison culture we are all exposed to in the media. Celebrity influencers showing off their multi-million-dollar homes have never been so popular, but few of us have the homes or budgets to match our fascination; creating something similar is simply out of the reach of most people. This gap between reality and

aspiration can really add to the sense of dissatisfaction, or even FOMO - fear of missing out. And what about all the home-makeover shows? As a society we love a transformation and yes they can be really inspiring and provide us with lots of juicy ideas. However, the problem with just focusing on the before and after pictures in these television programmes and magazines, is that the thought process and conversations between the designer and the client are often missing, not to mention what happens after the camera stops rolling. And it is the process behind the scenes that underlies the design choices that I want to share with you. To be a good home interior designer, it is important to know not just what, but why.

The good news is that there is another way, and this book is proof of it. I truly believe that now is your time to feel free to express yourself. Time to put your own feelings, views, and tastes before what's in fashion and 'on trend'! Time to create the home that's right for you - not a replica of the house that you saw on Instagram. As a designer, I love the fact that people are so different. There are a million ways and more for you to express yourselves. In this book, I will show you how to understand yourself and your own unique personality, so that you can choose just the right interiors and create the perfect home for your needs. I will guide you through a journey of self-discovery, at the end of which you'll find you have created the beautiful home you've always dreamt of. The best part is that you will have designed it yourself. All I will have done is give you a helping hand so that you know what to do. My philosophy is that a good designer should never take over this personal process of self-discovery or tell you what to do. After all it's your home, and you need to live in it and love it!

This book will 'open your eyes'!

Much of our response to our environment is instinctive and unconscious. I aim to make you super conscious of what you love and what you hate, so that creating the perfect home for you becomes super easy, instinctive, and fun to do. Yay!

As you work your way through this book, you will gradually gain more confidence in, and understanding of, your taste in interiors. My aim for those of you who are lacking in confidence is that as you build knowledge and awareness, you will feel validated that your true taste and preferences are not only brilliant, but perfect for you! You can then use your newfound confidence in design to create a space that really suits you and makes you happy. When people lose the need for external validation, they know what to do because it feels right to them. That is the power of this process.

This book has been written for those of you who want to live in a lovely home but really have no idea what you're doing when it comes to decorating it. This book is also for interior designers and interiors enthusiasts who have a lot of knowledge and confidence in designing interiors but want to understand more about the link between personality and interior design, psychology of space and sensory design. And it's for all those people who love interiors and also happen to love a good personality quiz! Don't worry, I've got you all covered!

It's time to put down the magazine, stop scrolling through social media images, and ignore the urge to copy-cat. Remember. You are an individual. Unique. And in personality terms there is no better way to be. You are perfect just as you are. Let's do this!

Michelle

Foreword

by Dr. Libby Sander

Our physical environments affect us profoundly. Our homes, especially so. Research, including my own, has highlighted the ways in which spaces influence our thinking, our mood, the way we connect with others and our wellbeing.

In a world where cities are increasingly noisy, homes are becoming smaller, and our lives more stressful; the need for well-designed spaces that support our lifestyle and who we are is more critical than ever. In research with my colleagues, after just eight minutes of exposure, we found a causal relationship between open-plan office noise and both stress and negative mood.

Designing spaces that reduce noise and enhance our connection with nature is essential to human health. Humans have an innate need to be connected with nature. Bringing nature into our homes can help reduce stress and increase creativity and focus. Just being able to see nature has been shown to increase both self-esteem and mood, particularly among younger people.

Looking at nature can cause the brain to shift into a different mode of processing. Researchers studied brain scans of people who were randomly assigned to look at pictures of a green meadow or a concrete roof for 40 seconds. Even this brief glimpse of nature was enough to shift the brain into a more relaxed mode. Other experiments and studies that included sounds of running water and forest smells also show that exposure to nature not only improved subjective measures of stress, but also physiological factors like heart rates and blood pressure.

When they are thoughtfully designed, our homes can promote psychological and emotional detachment from work. This is so important, even more so in an era of rising work from home rates following the Covid-19 pandemic. Taking a break on your favourite couch or in a sunny spot during the workday is an important part of maintaining a sense of wellbeing and helps your productivity levels. It's not something to feel guilty about.

Well-designed spaces make us feel psychologically safe. Our homes should be a refuge that allow us to retreat from distraction to restore ourselves mentally and physically.

Research on neuroarchitecture by Julio Bermudez found that just sitting people in certain types of buildings will automatically induce a mindful, meditative state. So much simpler than following gurus or spending hours trying to meditate battling intrusive thoughts over what we should have for dinner and whether we replied to that email required.

In this timely book, Michelle uses her extensive knowledge and experience of people and design to help us design spaces that support our physical, mental and emotional well-being.

By showing us how to understand our individual personality, Michelle reveals how to use layout, design, materials and colours to create bespoke spaces that work for us.

Whether you are thinking about just rearranging a room, or planning an entire remodel or new build, Michelle will guide you using evidence and best practice to design a space that you can't wait to spend time in.

Libby

Dr Libby Sander
Assistant Professor, Bond University, Queensland, Australia.

Libby is an acknowledged expert on the future of work, and a leading authority on the design of the workplace and its influence on thinking, emotion and performance.

She is Assistant Professor of Organisational Behaviour at Bond University, a Fellow of the Australian Institute of Management, the founder of Rethink and founder and director of the Future of Work Project.

Chapter 1

Your Dream home

"A home is not only a place, but also a feeling of belonging, of being in tune with ourselves."

This was a finding from the Danish happiness institute. Do you agree? In 2019 their researchers surveyed 13,000 people from ten countries across Europe on how they live and how they feel about their homes. They found that how we feel about where we live is actually much more important to our general happiness than might have been expected.

In fact, it turned out that 73% of people who are happy with their home are also happy in general. The research showed that a happy home is just as important as physical and mental health when it comes to people's overall happiness and is even more important to our overall happiness than income, employment, relationship status, whether or not we have children and many other life conditions.

So, with that in mind, how would you describe your dream home?

Your 'Dream home'

Take a moment and close your eyes. Take a few deep breaths. Keeping your eyes closed, imagine yourself in an idyllic home where you feel totally at ease and happy. This is your imagination. So, forget about any real-world impediments such as money, location and responsibilities. For the moment put them to one side and let your imagination dream.

A hint of Hollywood

Engage all your senses in this process. What can you hear? What kind of noises? Perhaps it's quiet, or maybe you hear the sound of children laughing. Can you hear birdsong? Or the sound of sea waves? Maybe you're a city lover; if so, can you hear the noise of people chattering and of traffic and machinery? What can you smell? Fresh air? Floral scents evocative of flower gardens or hedgerows? Maybe you can smell vanilla and warm sponge rising from the oven in your large country kitchen.

Pause... and take a moment to fully immerse yourself in this experience. Turn all of your senses up to full volume, scent and emotion.

Okay. Have you noticed that I helped you to imagine your dream home by accessing senses of sound and scent? Well, now it's time to visualise. Close your eyes again and return to your dream home. Where are you and what can you see? How big is your house? Do you know the style and era of this home? What about the location? Is it in the city, suburbs, countryside or wilderness? Maybe it's by the sea? Or in the mountains? Is it large and grand or small and rustic? What is the season? How warm are you? Let your imagination go on a journey. What do you find on that journey?

Pause ... and again give yourself a few moments to enjoy your imagination before coming back to the page.

Great! How did that feel? I love questions like these because they open up our minds to possibility. What did you imagine?

Try to think your experience through in detail and how it made you feel.

Everyone I do this exercise with imagines something different. Some people are able to go into amazing detail whereas other people are a bit stumped. Don't worry if you fall into the latter category as we have plenty of time to fill in the blanks for you as I guide you through this book. Some people come up with more than one home, and that's okay of course. After all, some people do have more than one home and many of us enjoy going on holidays to different locations as well as visiting with friends and family. Few of us spend time in only one environment. Here are four very different dream homes: a rural cottage, a city penthouse, a Hollywood modern mansion, and a Caribbean beach house. I've picked these to show the diversity of what we like and what we may be dreaming of. Are any of them similar to your dream house?

Three very different dream homes; mountain cottage, city apartment and tropical beach

You may be wondering how you can ever afford the home of your dreams, but this is not an exercise designed to fill you with frustration; it is an exercise designed to help you understand how your dream home makes you feel and what elements of home design make you happy. Some of those elements can be brought into the reality of your day-to-day life right now. We will revisit this in more depth in chapter 13 when we discuss how to pull happy memories into your home design.

How to use this book

This book is written in a format which is designed to be easy to pick up and put down. In each chapter I will take you through different aspects of personality and explain what that means for you and your 'ideal' interiors. We will look at case studies of real people living real lives and in each chapter you will be invited to take part in a short quiz designed to shed light on that aspect of your personality. There's a summary sheet for quiz notes at the end of chapter 2, and more resources throughout the book. So, by the time you reach the end of the book, you will have a full set of notes revealing your personality and design preferences.

I suggest that you work through the book step by step from front to back to gradually build up a picture of your personality and interiors tastes.

A free PDF design personality summary sheet and other resources are available for download from my website www.lightandfrank.com. You can download it as many times as you like.

We all deserve to be healthy and feel happy. Our homes are a huge part of this. You deserve a home designed to be perfect for you. Let's get started!

Chapter 2

What is Personality at Home?

I changed career in my mid 40s from HR management to interior design. It was both scary and exciting to learn a new profession from scratch but actually I found that a lot of skills and knowledge from my HR and corporate experience was relevant for my new career too, which was pretty reassuring.

I have a first degree in psychology, where understanding how individuals are different in terms of values, motivation, and learning styles is very relevant to the business of employing people. At first glance psychology didn't seem relevant to the world of interiors. In the lectures, assignments and reading the aesthetics and practicalities were paramount and what worked or didn't work was determined by a few tastemakers and experts.

Knowledge areas and careers are often siloed. We study together and work together in our subject areas and there isn't much cross-pollination between professional groups. As I learned quickly and started to work with clients, I had an instinct that there was more here to discover and wondered if there were any experts who were knowledgeable about the psychology of interiors? I was also curious to find out if quality research had been conducted to understand how humans react to the built environment and where it could be found? The answer to my search is the field of Environmental Psychology.

Environmental Psychology occupies the subject space where behavioural sciences and the architecture or the

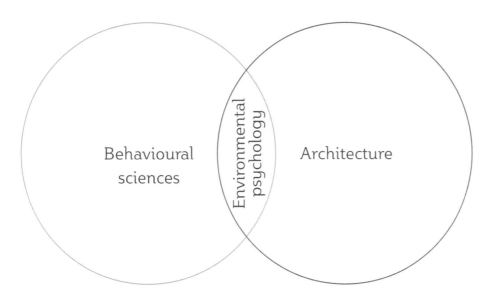

Where Environmental Psychology fits

design of our built environment meet. The British Psychological Society describes Environmental Psychology as "a distinct and recognised area of psychology... [focused] on the transactions between people and places."

A notable example where environmental psychologists, architects and designers have worked together to create an amazing space is a Dutch dementia village called 'Hogewey' where residents live in a protected environment that has been designed to resemble a village where they can shop, visit cafes, garden, do crafts, and pray. The village has extremely high security but, crucially, feels open because of the inner courtyards and the fact that people can wander freely. The space is designed around the patients' changed needs and perceptions. People with dementia have more difficulty with

things like colour perception and way finding. Other exceptional examples of how environmental psychology informs design include the field of sensory design where designers create spaces adapted for people with sensory impairments and some designers specialise in creating spaces for people with physical and emotional disabilities.

Environmental psychology is not as widely known about as it could be, especially when it comes to the popular subject of residential interiors. Such a shame, because, when we consider individuals and individual differences at a deeper level, the resulting design solutions can have a profound and positive impact on the space user.

An important element of psychology in design is understanding individual personalities and the needs of different personality types. I hear interior designers talking about personality and design all the time and I wonder what the word personality means to them. The word personality can be used in various ways: for example, "What a personality!" when referring to someone who is a strong character; or "This restaurant has real personality" when referring to atmosphere; or "Her clothes reveal her quirky personality" when talking about somebody's dress sense.

Personality is such a well-used word: but in this book I will use it in just two ways; both in a broad way, i.e. to describe someone's character, and, in a specific way, to describe an individual's personality traits. More on what personality traits are shortly.

As humans we have been gifted with five senses, differences in perception, individual brain wiring and different personalities. And we can all potentially benefit from understanding ourselves in relation to our environment.

In *Your Design Personality at Home* you will find a combination of concepts and ideas gleaned from research in subject areas including: environmental psychology, individual differences, psychometrics, social and behavioural psychology, historical architecture, anthropology, and colour psychology. I have, in addition, added my own ideas, conclusions, and advice. I invite you to read this book with a critical mind and create the answers that you are looking for. I have included a list of books and other reading in Chapter 18 for those of you that are interested in delving further into any of the subjects raised.

The basis of the 'Discover Your Design Personality' approach

As you read each chapter I'll take you through a fun and hopefully enlightening process. This is the same process I use when I work with a client on a design for a residential

It's important to emphasise that there are no right or wrong answers when discussing personality. And there are no traits that are better or worse than others.

The questions in this book are intended as a fun, informative yet informal quiz, not a validated psychometric tool. I have developed the questions that I think will best encourage readers' self-exploration and understanding.

Formal psychological testing is designed to provide objective measures of one or more psychological characteristics.

The most important feature of psychological tests is that they produce measures obtained under standardised conditions which have known reliability and validity (i.e. they provide a reliable and appropriate way of comparing one person's performance against others). (Ref: BPS website 31.12.2020)

If you want to explore personality testing in more depth, some information about test providers has been included at the back of this book.

Luxuriate in a bath at Heath House Hideaway Airbnb

space and in workshops I run online and in person.

In the 'Discover Your Design Personality' process we will explore and discover your individual take on the big five personality traits, your dominant moods and senses as well as the impact of your family background, values and beliefs on what you like and dislike.

In addition, I have added specific questions linked to the design subjects of colour, styles, forms and shapes, and then linked them back to your personality preferences. Here's a brief explanation of each in turn.

Big five personality traits

Psychologists in the 20th century including Allport, Eysenck and Cattell developed trait theory to describe the way people's characters are expressed, and how we differ from each other in terms of thoughts, feelings and behaviours. Our

personality traits are fairly fixed; as opposed to our state, which can change with altered moods and circumstances. Traits are thought to be fixed for us from early adolescence onwards. Put simply, that means that, whatever goes on in your environment, your level of sociability, need for order, and curiosity, etc, stays constant.

A number of personality models have been developed and the five traits we will go through in the book are based on the Big 5 or OCEAN model of personality. In 1985 Costa and McCrae developed the OCEAN model which stands for Openness, Conscientiousness, Extrversion, Agreeableness and Neuroticism. Each of us will have a unique 'score' on these traits and, when the scores are combined, it creates a unique profile of our personality. Think of a continuum or scale with high scorers at one end and low scorers at the other. The quizzes in this book are short and designed to give you a good level of understanding and awareness of where you score on each personality trait. They are not fully validated psychometric tests. (See notes at end of chapter.)

Our trait scores all have an impact on our environmental preferences but not to the same degree. The first three, extraversion, conscientiousness, and openness to experience have a big impact on people's interiors tastes. The final two, agreeableness and neuroticism, have some impact but less so.

Other factors

We will also explore your preferred moods and what environmental styles suit different moods. Then we will look at which of your five senses you prefer to use when experiencing your environment. Following that, the values exercise will reveal what is important to you at a deep level, and we will explore your early environmental experiences. There are so many clues to our personality and taste preferences and I want to include them all for you.

Learning about your own personality helps to build self-awareness. I think that this is one of the keys in life to finding happiness as a human in a fast paced and sometimes challenging world. If you know yourself well, you can make choices that suit you in terms of people, task and environment. You can place yourself in the situations that best suit you and help you thrive. And you are better informed to be able to avoid those that don't.

How does personality influence someone's taste in interiors?

Each of the traits and factors we will explore will reveal a preference for how you, me, and everyone else prefers their interiors. Whether someone describes themselves as a colour lover, or a fan of neutrals, will link back to their personality traits. And if someone loves minimalism or maximalism, guess what? Yes, you've got it, it will link back to their personality traits.

In our homes we reveal much about our personality in the way that we decorate. There are so many clues in all that you let people see: that favourite holiday snap, family photographs, artwork, plants. Even how you arrange your furniture will reveal how sociable and agreeable you are. If you know yourself well, you will have created an environment which really suits you. But what if you haven't? Or you aren't satisfied? Don't worry! This book will help you understand why, and what to do about it.

If there is one take-away or bottom line to this book it's this. Know that it's ok to be 'YOU' with your mind, your taste, your preferences and your personality. There are no right and wrong ways to 'BE' as long as you aren't hurting anyone. The choices you make about your environments will influence how happy you and those around you are. Do you want to buy a purple velour sofa? Go for it! Want a minimalist all white, marble-topped kitchen? Do it!

Is it really possible to create environments that promote wellness, creativity and happiness? As well as personal validation, there is a deeper and more meaningful side to this approach to Interior Design: our physical and emotional health.

A good environment that has been designed for us, uplifts us, makes us happier, more creative, more productive ,and more comfortable, both physically and emotionally.

However, when we spend time in places that do not suit us, it negatively affects our stress levels (heart rate, cortisol levels and blood pressure). The knock-on impact is lowered mood, sense of well-being and productivity. This is why I think it's so important to uncover what your individual needs are. By creating the interior that suits your personality, you are not only doing something nice for yourself, but you are also doing something that is essential for your health and wellbeing. That's why I'm so passionate about making this subject popular.

Are you ready to find out more? Let's dive in!

In the next five chapters we will discuss and discover your personality trait scores in a fun and informal way. As you work through each chapter there is an opportunity to stop and take notes. On the next page is a diagram to help you make sense of it all. When you have read all the chapters and done the quizzes you will have ALL of the

Michelle Armitage

ingredients to form a full picture of your personality preferences for Interiors.

You may decide to read this book and do these exercises with a partner or friend. I encourage you to do it separately to start with. When we live with other people, it's easy to be influenced by their views. Once you have completed everything, it'll be really interesting to share with them, but for now, try to do it on your own.

There is one exception to this and that is for Chapter 13. Although the questions are designed to bring happy memories flooding back, recalling early experiences can be quite an emotional process, so it's nice to do it with a partner or close friend.

	Area of personality		
Big Five	Highly open to experience, traditional, bit of both		
	Conscientious, easy-going, bit of both		
	Extrovert, introvert, bit of both		
	Agreeable, tough minded, bit of both		
	Emotionally stable or more sensitive		
Preferred moods	Write down your 5 words		
Values	Write down your key values		
Sensory dominance	Visual		
	Auditory		
	Taste/Smell		
	Kinaesthetic		
Colour palette preference	Brights	Mids	Darks
Favourite colour combination is			
Style preferences are			
Family memories	Evocative design elements to include		
Aha moments Further insights			

Actions/ideas:
What might you do now at home and work?
What are your short term and long term plans for improvement?

I am/ prefer to be	Design ideas and thoughts

Pastel	Muddy	Neutral

Design elements to avoid

Chapter 3

Extroversion & Introversion.
The energy trait

Is this an extroverts' paradise?

The open plan home was first dreamed of in the 1960s and it is still popular today. I'd like you to think of a large family-friendly kitchen/diner, where Mum or Dad are cooking and the kids are doing their homework or playing, whilst the family dog snoozes on a comfortable bed. They are all together in one large space. Then, maybe, you imagine opening the bifold doors out onto yet more space, and discover an extensive patio with large rattan sofas arranged around a coffee table, perhaps a BBQ or chimenea to the side and a drinks area. Welcome to the home of the extrovert; where everything can be seen and done together. No one need ever be alone again. Is this Utopia?

Understanding differences

It may be heaven for some people, but what I have described would be a kind of hell for others. If you are considering an extension or knocking a wall down, my advice to you is to be careful. Before you make any changes to your space, it is a good idea to think about all your functional needs first. In modern houses today most rooms are multipurpose. Have you thought about who uses the space(s) the most, for what, and at what time of day? You probably think that more space can only be a positive thing, but do you know how your extension, or having more open space, will help you as an individual or family?

A yellow front door is a bright and vibrant welcome for a visitor

Open plan living

In fact, more open space isn't always better. Consider that sometimes, individuals need somewhere to retreat to so that they can have privacy or be alone. They might want to either be quiet, for example, when meditating or practising yoga, or they might want to be noisy playing musical instruments or playing games online. And some personalities need that quiet and solitude more than you may realise. This is particularly important for families, where the children are growing older. Whilst open plan is often ideal for living with little ones, the picture changes considerably when parents are living with teenagers.

If you are considering structural changes in your home it really pays to take time to think about whether you and your family are introvert, extrovert, or a mix of both, and what that means for your collective needs on an environmental, emotional and structural space level.

Trait definition

This personality factor has two ends of the spectrum that probably feel familiar to you: extroversion and introversion. These terms were popularised by Carl Jung, a psychologist from the early 20th Century and are now in common language use. But what do they mean?

People high in extroversion tend to seek out opportunities for social interaction, where they are often known as the 'life of the party.' They are comfortable with others, gregarious, and prone to action rather than contemplation. Whereas people low in extroversion are more likely to be people "of few words," those who are quieter, introspective, reserved and thoughtful.

Most people tend to think of extroversion only in terms of sociability or social confidence. However, that's not quite right. Extroverts can enjoy spending time on their own and introverts are not shy. In fact many are very socially confident; just think of a few self-proclaimed introverts that are accomplished actors and singers. This trait isn't just about levels of sociability; it goes deeper than that. I think it's most helpful to think about what environmental situations people find energising or draining than just whether someone enjoys socialising or not.

Neuroscientists have found a difference in the way that introverts' and extroverts' brains are wired. Eysenck was a pioneer of this biological basis to personality theory in the late 1960s. He showed that some people had different levels of cortical arousal in the brain even when presented with the same stimulus. Human beings need cortical arousal for wakefulness, vigilance, muscle tone, heart rate and other important bodily functions. Whilst introverts prefer a limited external amount of stimulus, extroverts need a lot more stimulus to result in the same optimal 'internal' level of arousal. And this is beyond people's relationships and socialising; it is related to our external world. For example; a walk on a summer's day, sunbathing on a busy beach, or the response to the way a space is organised and decorated are all examples of different levels of environmental stimulation.

So, understanding yourself in this way, is very helpful when we consider what is the ideal physical environment for an introvert or extrovert. An extrovert is more likely to like strong colours, busy patterns, more objects to look at, more movement and activity, fast beat sounds to listen to, and brighter lights when compared to an introvert.

The images overleaf show this difference beautifully. The colour palette is very similar: black, white, and pink. But the rooms couldn't be more different! Lisa has designed a room with clean lines, pale or white colours, limited objects, tidy storage (objects hidden away). A calm, light-filled room with space to think. This desk is a place for quiet work. A real sanctuary. Perfect for a child with an introverted personality.

On the other hand, Marcie has designed a space beautifully suited to extroverts. Her lounge is very stimulating with lots of patterns including busy and dramatic dark wallpaper and a leopard print coffee table. This lounge is perfectly designed to help extroverts feel happy. It's a space that

Left: A calming child's bedroom by Lisa Riddock

Below: A lounge for a sociable extrovert by Marcie Kobernus

will spark conversation and lift energy. I can imagine wine or coffee and lots of chatter and laughter in this room. Can you?

Thinking of whether a room design will work for an extroverted or introverted personality really helps when you are trying to determine the desired mood and energy levels. And design is not just about visual elements. Music and sounds of nature are known to support mood maintenance or stimulate a mood change and all the other senses can impact mood powerfully too. We will come on to talk more in depth about senses and sensory design in Chapter 9.

The examples I have just shared have two different purposes: a bedroom and a lounge. In most of our homes each room has multiple functions, and we often need to be flexible about the way we use space. But the main purpose of a bedroom is sleep, and the main purpose of a lounge is to either relax or be sociable. So, in addition to the functional and mood needs of a space, I advise you to layer in personality needs too, so that ALL your needs can be met in terms of design style.

The character traits of extroversion and introversion are extremes on a continuum. And It's worth noting that although someone is mostly extroverted, they may want a calm bedroom which will help them to wind down before they go to sleep. And conversely, another person may have a vibrant, colourful and exciting kitchen/diner where they do all their socialising and family activities. The rest of their house feels more neutral and pared back to suit their introverted preferences of calmer activities and a calmer vibe. It's okay and often a good idea to create different feels in the rooms of your house to suit your functional needs, individual personality and your dominant mood. I realise that you may think this runs contrary to the idea of a 'red thread' that many designers talk about when designing their homes, but it need not if that's what you want. I'll discuss the concept of the red thread more at the end of the book in Chapter 16 – Next steps.

Quiz time!

From the descriptions and the two examples above, you may have an idea already where you fit on this personality trait before we look at the full definition, but let's do a quiz to help you to see yourself clearly. Answer the following questions fairly quickly. Try not to think too hard about your answer. We'll analyse your answers at the end.

Please read the following statements and mark whether you agree or disagree.

1   I like to be the centre of attention.

2   I prefer playing team games than playing on my own.

3   I love meeting new people.

4   I love talking about ideas and telling stories.

5   I find it really easy to make new friends.

6   I get bored if I spend too much time on my own.

7   I open up to people straight away. I have few or no secrets.

8   I find speaking in public easy to do.

9   I like nothing more than to bounce ideas off people and get their feedback.

10 I love to be the host, and often invite friends over for dinner.

Your results!

Mostly agree

The answers you gave in this process suggest that you have an extroverted personality. This means that you gain energy from social situations and from exploring your physical environment.

In the physical environment your high need for stimulation means that you are more likely to like bright and bold colours. Those colours are known as fully saturated and are either pure or mixed with only the smallest amount of another colour or black, white and grey. You will also like bright, busy and colourful patterns and this may include lots of stimulating art on the walls. You may also enjoy dramatic lighting and a music system that you can play energising sounds on. You like to see ornaments, plants, vases, bowls, flowers, objects of interest, trinkets, etc, more than others. All of this counts towards stimulus in your environment. This energises you to the right level and that makes you happy.

Your home needs to reflect your love of socialising and being busy. In the home the kitchen and dining areas are opportunities to hold social gatherings. You love open-plan design where you can see all the activities in the home going on at once. Your furniture is arranged in a friendly way with seating facing towards each other; this supports social activity, and makes interactions and conversations easy.

The garden is another great opportunity space for social gatherings. Again, you prefer an open space where you can see everything at once.

Some psychologists like to discuss and argue definitions and what is and isn't part of a trait like extroversion. Some extrovert traits include a desire for status and ambition. If you are a relaxed, slightly messy person, and like people to feel comfortable and at home, then it is likely that 'status' is not part of your extroverted nature. However, if you enjoy luxury goods or handmade artisan furniture, or perhaps a collection of valuable paintings, then you might be an extroverted home-owner who likes to 'show off' these items. Thus, status is a part of your extraversion and showing off is important to you. And you are likely to have similar friends. There is nothing wrong with wanting to show off. Remember, we are looking without judging. We will talk about status again in Chapter 12.

The questions and definitions in this book are a deliberately 'light touch' approach, designed to raise self-awareness in a fun way. There are many personality tests that you can buy on the market which are similar to each other, and most, if not all, are of a high quality. If you are interested in taking one, do check that it has a good reputation with the British Psychological Society before you buy.

Equal mix of agree and disagree

You may be what is known sometimes as an ambivert: meaning you are both introvert and extrovert. Or you may be unusual and have extreme scores and exist at both ends of the continuum at once. This means that you are really sociable sometimes, but also need to spend a lot of quiet time alone. If you are in the middle, you have the benefit of being able to see and feel both sides of this trait. This means that you are then able to be more flexible and adapt easily and comfortably to more social situations; and you feel comfortable in a wider variety of environments than most people.

Please read both of the other descriptive paragraphs and pick out the elements that reflect you and your needs.

There are different elements within the trait of extroversion such as dominance, warmth, and privateness. You may be high in some areas but lower in others. Each of the big five factors can be split into different facets. Sometimes a middle score will mean a middle score on all the facets or a high score on some facets and a very low score on others.

Mostly disagree

The answers you gave in this process suggest that you have an introverted personality type. This means that you gain energy from within and need time for quiet time and reflection, away from others. Your mind already has a lot going on and too much socialising with others, or time spent out and about, can be draining. Time spent alone is where you charge your batteries.

In the physical environment, you are more likely to like quiet, order and serenity. This often leads to a visual preference for neutral or harmonious paint schemes, simpler or no patterns on fabrics and walls; a pared back look that is clean and smells fresh and a space that has good sound management. The key for you is a design style that gives you the right level of stimulus without being overwhelming. Clutter can be annoying, so you tend to avoid having too many objects. Art and objects you do display in your home are chosen sparingly and carefully.

When you need to hold a lot of stuff in a space, good storage may solve this problem. For example you might have a lot of materials needed to do a hobby. With good storage you can hide it out of sight. Bright lights, loud sounds and strong smells can also be more annoying for you than others. All these factors need to be considered when creating an interior for you.

As an introvert, you need to have plenty of space for quiet reflection in your home. Interior walls are important for separated activity and you would rather have separated spaces than open plan. You also prefer lighting to be subtle and subdued and furniture arrangements to be simple.

You will lay out your furniture to suit your own activities, rather than those that include lots of others. Introverts tend to have a few close friends they know well rather than lots of friends. As a result, furniture arrangements often suit solitary or smaller more intimate gatherings.

Garden design is another opportunity for you to create spaces for quiet reflection. A water feature might create soothing sounds, and also be a helpful way to mask unwanted neighbour noise. Use your planting schemes for beauty but also for creating a sense of privacy. You will prefer gardens with separate areas and perhaps secret or private spaces, rather than an open design where everything can be seen at once. Remember to create auditory privacy as well as visual privacy; tall plants are especially helpful in achieving this.

Personality summary

The factors associated with extroversion are: sociable, assertive, outgoing, energetic, talkative, articulate, fun-loving, affectionate, friendly, and socially confident. The elements associated with introversion are: quiet, cerebral, withdrawn, independent, solitary, considered, unassuming, subtle, thoughtful, reflective, serious, good listener.

A bias in western culture

In many countries, especially in Europe and North America, it seems that extroverts are more valued by society and open plan homes and offices dominate because they suit the extrovert. One example is schools: designed with large open classrooms which inevitably lead students to create a lot of activity and noise. There are many examples like this, where society is biased to suit extroverts and, as a result, it's sometimes a strain for introverts who are trying to survive in environments they find overstimulating and uncomfortable.

In Susan Cain's exceptional book 'Quiet', she explores what it's like for introverts living in a world dominated by extroverts. Her book aims to shed light on the bias in society against introverts and gives permission to introverts, to spend time alone without feeling guilty about it! One of the aims of her book is to encourage society to design workplaces and schools to suit both introverts and extraverts. This is so important for learning, inclusion and workplace performance, I couldn't agree more! It's time we appreciated individual differences and created public environments that suit all personality types. Everyone deserves to inhabit environments in which they will thrive.

Design tips for extroverts

I've thought through what will help people with personality results that are at either end of this continuum. Here are some top tips to help you create the home that reflects your true nature.

- Be bold in your decisions at home! For you 'the more the merrier' is true. Express yourself. Don't hold back. If you are nervous of doing this, build it up gradually at first. For example, start with a bold painting, then a rug, maybe a new chair,

finally a change of paint scheme and window treatment? Add more and more layers of change as your confidence grows and stop when you are satisfied.

- Create rich and sensory spaces that maximise stimulus for all of your five senses, at the right level for you.

- Set your home up for hosting small and larger gatherings. This is something you probably love to do. Look at the space in your home where people gather. Evaluate the space and the furniture. Does it work? Does it support human

A lounge for an introvert

interaction? Chairs placed at 90-degree angles to each other work best for this. Do areas flow well? How can you open out the furniture layout? Do you need to change or remove some furniture? Would a wall knocked down create better flow in your home?

- Be sensitive that not everyone has the same preference as you. When you have introverted friends visiting, consider how you might make your home more comfortable for them. This might be as simple as letting them sit with a view of your garden rather than a busy indoor space.

- Creating a workspace that helps you to be productive will need some stimulus such as: background noise (music or light chatter), objects on your desk, or items of interest around you. You are likely to resist any 'clear desk' policy an organisation tries to impose on you!

Design tips for introverts

- Know that it's ok to want your own calmer space and ask for it. Make sure you have quiet space to retreat to.

- Create a space that manages or minimalises stimulus for all five senses at the right level for you.

- Choose pastels and neutral shades for decoration. Add in the odd pop of brightest colour or not, to your own preference.

- Opt for simpler lines when choosing furniture. Avoid scrolls and frills.

- Don't knock down all your walls in your home. Allow walls for separation, little nooks of intimate spaces and separate activities.

- Arrange your furniture so that conversations are less 'full' on, e.g. place your chairs side by side or at 90 degrees rather than opposite each other. These arrangements will suit you best.

- Invest in sound insulation to minimise sound becoming too loud within your home. There is more information on this in Chapter 9. Know and use the objects that help reduce sound levels within the home. For example, carpet, curtains, soft furnishings and plants all help to reduce noise in the home.

- Ensure you buy a property away from a main road, train line or flight path, and visit the streets at different times of days to pick up clues about local activity and noisy neighbours. You may think that everybody wants this, but as an introvert, you will be more bothered by this when compared to other people.

- Use window treatments such as frosted glass, shutters and blinds to create good visual privacy.

- Create a work-space that helps you to be productive. It should be orderly, uncluttered, solitary and above all

totally quiet. You need to be able to be free of interruptions too. Avoid the open plan office where possible. It is your worst nightmare, because you cannot concentrate amongst all the activity and chatter.

Exercise

Now we have completed your first quiz it is time for you to write up some notes in your summary sheet in Chapter 2. Find your sheet and answer the following questions.

- What answers did you find?

- Where are you on this trait? High, medium or low?

- What has this meant for environments that you've enjoyed spending time in, and environments where you have really felt uncomfortable?

- What design thoughts or ideas did the chapter or quiz raise?

Chapter summary

In this chapter we explored the first personality trait of the Big Five.

We learned that, environmentally, extroverts prefer open plan spaces and open layouts, long views, lots of stimulus and things to look at, bold colours, activity, and noise. We also discovered that introverts prefer privacy, separated spaces, few objects, simpler spaces, quiet, muted colours, and above all, less stimulus. You have started the journey to understanding your personality in relation to interior design!

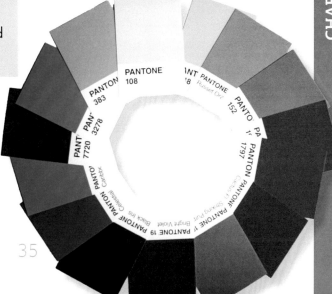

Chapter 4

Conscientious.
The Orderly Trait

What is conscientiousness?

Do you remember the Mr Men books? Perhaps you read them as a child, or read them to your children now? I have happy memories of my dad reading them to me when I was little. Arthur Lowe was the TV narrator for the Mr Men stories at the time, and my dad is a great mimic of Arthur's deep, low and gravelly-voiced tones. Our favourite was Mr Messy. In the story he meets two men who cleaned up his cottage, and then they cleaned him up too! Their catch phrase was, "Tidy and neat, neat and tidy!" When I started to write this chapter, it's the first example I thought of. They epitomised characters with what is known in personality theory as 'high conscientiousness'.

How ordered and tidy are you? Let's picture a scenario that might help you know the answer straight away. You go out for a walk with a friend and her dog. Afterwards she invites you in for a cuppa. As you walk into her home the hallway gives you an instant sense of how disordered her life is. There's an overloaded coat rack groaning with coats and no room for your coat so you hang it on the banister. A shoe rack might once have been organised and tidy, but is now so overflowing with shoes that some have spilled onto the floor in a higgledy piggledy manner. There's a rug for stamping off mud from the walk and it is pretty muddy from previous walks. There's also a well-used towel to wipe the dog down; it's been thrown on the floor and clearly not picked up since the last walk.

How do you feel reading this description? Does it sound familiar and homely, or does it sound uncomfortably

A lovely floor-to-ceiling marble bathroom by Naomi Carroll

messy? The strength of your reaction to this description may give you a clue to your innate level of conscientiousness.

Trait definition

Conscientiousness is a trait that can be described as the tendency to enjoy planning and order in everyday life, and to control impulses and act in socially acceptable ways. Conscientious people excel in their ability to delay gratification, work within the rules, as well as plan and organise effectively. A person who is low in conscientiousness is much more likely to break the rules, procrastinate, work less hard, and be impulsive or spontaneous.

Do you know instinctively where you are on this continuum? Can you imagine how scores on this trait impact people in terms of day-to-day domestic living? How would you go about designing the ideal environment for someone who is high or low on this trait?

What is the ideal for you in your home? Do you have the kind of home where everything has its place? Or is it a home where you can see the evidence of many incomplete jobs and the resulting piles of clutter? How many half-finished jobs are still visible? How clean is the space? Can you see any dust? Not just on the table but what about the tops of the pictures or skirting boards? Kitchen surfaces are a big clue to the way people score on this personality trait. At one end of the continuum, nothing is visible; even the kettle and toaster are put away when not in use. At the other end of the continuum, you can hardly see the work surface for kitchen gadgets, jars, bowls of fruit, piles of post and, well, you get the picture.

Do you know someone who would be irritated by the untidiness in a neighbour's garden two doors away? For a tidy person, the sight of another person's untidiness feels like an insult. In my experience this trait can lead to lots of domestic disagreements about things like washing up and

whose turn it is to clean the loo, but you probably know that already, don't you?

A couple of interesting trends that are popular at the moment, are cleaning and de-cluttering. Social media 'influencers' extolling the virtues of being clean, tidy ,and regularly de-cluttering are plentiful and some have many fans and followers.

Sometimes society holds an ideal for us all to aspire to. A high level of conscientiousness appears to be one of those ideals. And if you are like that it's ok. But, if you're not into that, you might need a bit of support to feel ok too. Trying to live up to society's ideals can be very tiring. Like all the other areas we will discuss, being really tidy and organised is just a personality preference and it's actually also ok to be untidy and messy sometimes, or all of the time. Someone is not RIGHT because they like it clean and tidy. It's just a preference. Those of you that like order, tidiness and rules may be a little upset by this, but bear with me. I'm not asking YOU to change either!

There is a popular phrase 'tidy home, tidy mind' and a lot of well-meaning managers impose clear desk policies in workplaces. Hmmm... I wonder which personality type dreamed up those ideas?!

Being a bit messy and disorganised doesn't mean that you are less able, or less creative or even less productive. Interestingly, research has shown that the key to productivity and creativity is to have freedom to create the environment that works best for you. So that might mean a really tidy desk, or a very cluttered desk, or something somewhere in between.

Health warning: I'm not talking here about leaving rotting food on plates or hoarding rubbish or having piles and piles of old magazines and books and clothes. Even if you have a very low or high score this does not mean that you have obsessive compulsive disorder (OCD) or are a hoarder. These conditions are serious, potentially life-limiting medical conditions, and as such are outside the parameters of the quizzes within this book.

Alongside cleanliness, order, and tidiness in the home, planning is another aspect of the conscientious personality trait. Some people love to plan everything, whilst others prefer spontaneity. This will show up with the use of rotas, routines, planners on walls, etc, or, alternatively, having none of those things.

In design terms the way we use and store our possessions is really key to helping us feel comfortable in the space. And you probably guessed already that the design of, and the way you organise your 'stuff' and how you feel about it, is a big clue to your personality preference here. Few people know themselves well or have thought clearly about what their needs are. For example, ask yourself if you prefer things out of sight or on show? Are you happy to put things away in the loft or shed, or do you more regularly declutter and avoid this habit?

Devol's warm, rustic kitchen inspired by the feel of gentleman's haberdashery

Why not do a small audit of your space? How do you organise your bookshelves or kitchen cupboards? Do you think that you have enough storage? Do you have too little storage or too many possessions? How often do you have a clear out? In my experience, most individuals, couples and families would benefit from better storage solutions in their home and an annual or bi-annual sort out.

Most kitchens in magazines and showrooms are a good example of interiors that would suit someone with a high score in conscientiousness. They are carefully lit and styled with props and a stylist's know-how. The cabinets might be a simple design with clean lines, work surfaces are uncluttered or artfully styled; everything is clean and new, whilst food stuff is carefully and beautifully displayed. Don't be fooled into thinking these images reflect reality and compare yourself harshly. I recently watched a video tour of Hollywood actor Dakota Johnson's home. She had a full bowl of limes in her kitchen. Who needs twenty limes, I wondered? When interviewed about it on the Jimmy

Fallon show, she said, "Oh that was the stylist, I don't even like limes!"

Some kitchens that I walk into as a designer still look like the first day they were built, many years after they have been installed. I have to say though, the majority don't. Kitchens are busy places and not just used for cooking. They are spaces where people like to meet up to chat; surfaces are used as dumping grounds for post, keys, and handbag contents. When combined with dining rooms to create family areas they are also depositories for toys and all other kinds of stuff.

Clean and sleek kitchen

Quiz time!

From the above description you may have an idea already where you fit on this personality trait, but, before we look at the full definition, let's do a quiz to help you to see yourself clearly. Answer the following questions fairly quickly. Try not to think too much about your answer. We'll analyse the answers at the end.

Please read the following statements and mark whether you agree or disagree.

1   I try and do jobs carefully and get it right first time.

2   I like to follow rules. They are usually there for a good reason.

3   I strive for excellence in everything I do.

4   I have a cleaning routine at home and I stick to it.

5   I am a perfectionist.

6   Time-keeping is important to me.

7   I work hard to achieve my goals.

8   To be able to plan ahead is important to me.

9   Without standards, nothing would be done properly.

10 I find it hard to be spontaneous.

Your results!

Mostly agree

You are very conscientious and hard working in life. You like organisation, order and control. Everything in your home has a place and you like to keep things neat and tidy. Your books and CDs are likely to be in alphabetical (or an alternative and carefully-thought through) order. Your kitchen cupboards are regularly cleaned and always tidy. Open any storage in your home and we will see neatly-folded jumpers, jars facing out so you can see the label, and not a speck of dust anywhere. It's extremely unlikely that you will find any old products past their sell-by dates.

Your decoration standards are very high and good quality workmanship is very important to you. Chips of paintwork or a shabby 'cut in' bother you. You are likely to be house proud with a regular cleaning routine.

Any deviation from the above is bothersome to you. A harmonious home for you is a well-planned, well-maintained and organised home.

Equal mix of agree and disagree

You are fairly tidy and organised, but also flexible and can change plans and priorities sometimes. There are different elements within this trait such as planning, rules orientation and perfectionism, and you may be high in some areas but lower in others. Each of the big five factors can be split into different facets. Sometimes a middle score will mean a middle score on all the facets, or a high score on some facets and a very low score on others.

The benefit of being both organised and easy-going is that you are then able to be more flexible and adapt to more situations. You feel comfortable in a wider variety of environments than most people. Please read both of the other descriptive paragraphs and pick out the elements that best reflect you and your needs.

Mostly disagree

You are an easy-going/ lackadaisical person. You prefer either a little or a lot of chaos at home. Every day is an opportunity for changing things up, or being spontaneous. This is sometimes followed by procrastination. As a result, a happy home for you is one is a certain amount of unpredictability and chaos.

You enjoy spontaneity and will happily be distracted away from planned tasks or events. You may start jobs and get distracted, only coming across what you had started many hours later! As a result your home is likely to be filled with little piles of half-done activity.

You are not fastidious or particularly house-proud and will clean as and when it occurs to you. Or you may choose to delegate to a cleaner so that you don't have to think about it at all.

Entering very neat and tidy spaces might make you feel a little uncomfortable or uneasy.

Personality Summary

Elements within the high conscientiousness trait include: persistent, ambitious, thorough, self-disciplined, consistent, predictable, controlled, reliable, resourceful, hardworking, energetic, and a planner.

Those lower on this trait can be described as: flaky, easy-going, un-disciplined, spontaneous, freewheeling, inconsistent, lazy, relaxed and unpredictable.

Design tips for those high in conscientiousness

- Support yourself in your needs with efficient systems like regular cleaning routines, well planned storage, rotas and schedules.

- Choose materials for your interiors carefully, as ease of cleaning will be more important for you than most, e.g. choose fabrics that are stain proof and don't produce lint, carpets that don't show dirt, and kitchen surfaces that don't stain or easily mark.

- Ask for support in home maintenance and cleaning from others, even if

you think they don't do it as well as you (that's impossible!).

- Please try and understand that other people who live with you are not being rude or insensitive when they don't follow your high standards. They are living to their own standards quite happily. My advice is to try and find a way to compromise, so you can both relax. See Chapter 15 for more tips for couples.

Design tips for those low in conscientiousness

- Enjoy your home as it is and continue to live in a comfortable and relaxed way.

- When you do tidy up, try doing one room at a time to create a sense of completion and accomplishment.

- Create hidden storage where you can bundle things up out of sight when you want to.

- If you like lots of objects or books think about putting them in glass-fronted cabinets which are great at keeping things dust free.

- Even you can get overwhelmed when things pile up. Support yourself with some routines for cleaning and de-cluttering, so that you avoid feeling overwhelmed.

- If you like it cleaner than you are prepared to do yourself then you are the ideal client for a regular cleaner. If you can afford it, why not do it? There is no shame in asking for help with things you don't enjoy. Remember, some people enjoy cleaning!

- Try to have respect for those with higher standards than you when you live with them or visit them. Why not share the load by washing up, loading the dishwasher, wiping down surfaces or putting used socks in the laundry, if you live with someone more conscientious than you.

On the subject of de-cluttering

Depending on your personality you will have an optimum desired amount of possessions. One of the misconceptions about decluttering is that it always ends up with the goal of a sparse or minimalist interior. This is simply not true. Everybody collects possessions and rarely do we keep these items for our whole lives. At some point things need to either be given away, thrown away or sold. Those of you who scored highly on the trait of conscientiousness are more likely to clean thoroughly and have clear-outs on a regular basis. Here here are some tips on decluttering for those of you that don't do that; those of you with low levels of conscientiousness.

- My first advice is probably a bit surprising: I want you to be cautious about overzealous clear-outs. You may miss items (later on) if your clear-out is too ruthless which is counterproductive because it can make you wary of de-cluttering in the future.

- Before you start, have an idea of what you want your home to look like when you've finished. Perhaps you want clearer surfaces, or maybe tidier storage, or even more floor space?! Having a vision before you start will help you stay motivated during the process.

- Try an 'interim' de-clutter instead. The classic approach is to have 3 piles: the first is for items you will definitely keep, the second is for items that you definitely want to get rid of, but the third pile is the troublemaker. It's the 'I'm not sure' pile. The not sure pile creates inertia. Put those items out of sight in an airtight crate or box and put them somewhere secure and dry and diarise to review the crates after six months. If you don't have the space to store boxes at home, ask a friend or family member to put them in their garage or loft. When you get to the review, if you haven't missed an item, you will feel much more comfortable taking it to the charity shop. I hope this tip helps you feel more comfortable and less anxious about de-cluttering. Of course you have to remember to revisit the boxes after a few months.

- If these tips don't make you feel confident about decluttering, perhaps you could ask for help from someone you know who is more ruthless than you. Do you dare to do that?! If you need a gentler approach to being supported, I really recommend hiring the services of a professional de-clutterer. There is increasing evidence that de-cluttering is akin to therapy, in that it's hard to do, but once completed can be very emotionally freeing.

Exercise

Write up your quiz results and any additional notes in your summary sheet in chapter 2.

- What answers did you find?

- Where are you on this trait? High, medium or low?

- What has this meant for environments that you've enjoyed spending time in, and environments where you have really felt uncomfortable?

- What design thoughts or ideas did the chapter or quiz raise?

Chapter summary

In this chapter we explored the second personality trait of the Big Five: conscientiousness. We learned that environmentally, people who score high on conscientiousness prefer neatness, order, rules and systems. Cleaning routines are important to them, and spaces need to be easy to clean as a priority. Mess is upsetting and disruptive. They may prefer materials which look clean and shiny.

On the other hand, people who score lower on the trait of conscientiousness prefer spontaneity and reject routines. They don't notice mess as much as others. And they are much more comfortable within a chaotic environment.

Chapter 5

Openness to Experience.
The Creativity trait

Imagine a home where there is so much to look at, you do not know where to look first! There is an extensive and eclectic gallery of art and objects on the wall, different colours and patterns everywhere, bookshelves are groaning with books, and there are more books spilled into piles on the floor. You notice that there are lots of lamps, but none of the lamps match; they're all different shapes, colours, styles and sizes! The only thing that is small is the TV. It is dwarfed by everything else. You can see photographs, ornaments, vases, glassware, candlesticks, and a stuffed animal in the corner. So many curios and objects from what you assume are gifts or perhaps they are mementos from the homeowners own adventures and experiences. A map suggests a fondness for travel. You can see some wool, knitting needles, and a half-finished scarf abandoned on a chair. You also notice a sewing machine left out on the kitchen table surrounded by colourful and patterned material. Both of these activities suggest a love of making and creating. The floor is covered with rugs that slightly overlap and have varying patterns and designs. You cannot make out the wallpaper design because it is covered with framed pictures of art and photographs.

Welcome to the home of someone who scored high on the personality trait of openness to experience; a trait linked with a love of variety and creativity. How does this description make you feel? Are you excited to find out more or do you feel slightly overwhelmed even with just a description? The answer to these questions will give you a clue to your score on this personality trait.

The colourful inspiration of a Marrakech souk

Angie C tells me that she is a design junkie and compulsive wanderer These images of her farmhouse are a great example of a home full of variety and stimulus with layers of interest but, in a neutral palette. Often maximalism is associated with colour but as Angie expertly shows in her Texas home, it works very well in muted tones. I think Scout the dog approves, don't you?

Trait definition

Openness to experience concerns an individual's willingness to try new things, to be vulnerable, and the ability to think outside the box. A high scorer will enjoy novelty, uniqueness, abstract thinking, a wide variety of arts and entertainment, and new experiences. Whilst an individual who is low in openness to experience prefers more traditional décor and dress, routine over variety, tends to stick to what they know, and prefers a tangible 'down to earth' approach to all things.

Both types are valid remember. It's just as ok to want to go on holiday to somewhere familiar or order your favourite dish from your favourite restaurant as to enjoy exploring new places and tastes.

Understanding the trait in relation to choosing holidays and eating out makes sense but that's about experiences not homes. You may be wondering how their homes could look different? Actually, this aspect of personality is incredibly relevant in relation to home environment.

When you enter a room in the house of a high 'openness to experience' person, you will see evidence around you of all the many things they are interested in. They may have art or photographs in abundance. A book collection is a really good clue about what they enjoy. Look out for curios and objects from various adventures and experiences like travel. Sometimes there are a lot of bold colours and patterns too, but not always. Being a colour lover is more linked with extraversion than openness. Certainly, somebody who scores highly on both extraversion and openness will usually have a very visually busy, colourful and stimulating home.

Of course, not everyone is like this. Some people are quite the opposite and like a more traditional or tried and tested approach to life and home. A favourite meal or holiday destination is one where the repetition of the experience is what makes it so enjoyable. Clues to this type of person's home is trickier to see because it is the absence of change and newness that you are looking for. In terms of art and objects, conventional items will be

This vintage stall gives a hint of how a layered generational home might look with treasured objects collected over time.

preferred, although there are still quite a variety of styles available that might fall under the 'traditional banner.' For example, a Chesterfield armchair looks very different to a mid-century modern chair, yet both might be described as conventional or traditional. Someone more traditionally minded will probably also prefer what is known as representational art, where the painting closely resembles a photograph of a person, pet, still life, or landscape.

Why is getting your understanding of your environment in relation to this trait so important? Don't we all like the same art, ornaments or curios? The short answer is, no, we don't. And if we do like to fill our homes with objects, then the type of objects and décor and art that we choose will vary widely depending on our level of openness to experience. And when we don't want lots of objects to look at, that reveals our taste too.

An interesting aspect of personality is that, if we feel strongly about an aspect of our personality, it also becomes part of our identity. We are strongly attached to that part of ourselves. The spaces we choose,

and the objects we surround ourselves with, serve to reinforce our sense of self and this is an important part of creating the 'at home' feeling, which, in turn, increases our sense of safety. It's worth saying here that both high and low scorers on this trait might have a high need for safety. We will cover this subject more in Chapter 12 on values.

Describing what it means to have a traditional décor is somewhat difficult because the concept is a fluid one. Traditional décor has a timelessness about it, a form and style repeated over generations. In the U.K., where I am from, this might include items like wood panelling or elegant egg and dart covings, Chesterfield sofas, wingback chairs, symmetry, elegance, portraiture artwork, Persian rugs, dark, pastel or neutral paint choices. Your country will have its own traditions and favourites over the years.

Quiz time!

From the above descriptions you may have an idea already where you fit on this personality trait. Let's do a quick quiz to help you see yourself clearly. Answer the following questions quickly. Try not to think about your answers for too long. As usual, we will analyse your answers at the end.

Please read the following statements and mark whether you agree or disagree:

1   I like to try new things like foreign food.

2   The best thing about travel is experiencing new people and cultures.

3   I get bored easily.

4   As a child, I enjoyed games of make believe.

5   I am intrigued by patterns in plants and nature.

6   I have a wide range of hobbies and interests.

7   Aesthetic details are very important to me.

8   I have lots of books. I don't want to throw any away.

9   Sometimes I drive a longer way home, just for the variety.

10 I love all kinds of music.

Your results!

Mostly agree

You appreciate beautiful spaces and things; aesthetics are important to you. You also like to try new things and experiences. You are someone who is stimulated by many things including the arts, nature, and music. You love activities where you need to use your imagination. You are open to new innovations and like to try new styles and approaches. You are likely to own a lot of photos or art, books, and items that support creative pursuits such as photography, painting or cooking. Certainly, you like to pick up new things to add to your home, which is full of a variety of items collected from events, holidays, and days out. You like to mix up new and old objects, e.g, a Persian rug next to modern abstract art or a collection of clashing colours and patterns. If you enjoy travelling, it's likely that there will be evidence of different cultures and places you've been to. You enjoy so many different objects and items that, sometimes, it is a challenge to get them all to 'work' together. Now and then you will need to 'clear out' old purchases so that you can make space for new ideas and things. You do get bored by your environment from time to time, and want to change your décor more than most. Sometimes the itch for change can be met by rearranging rather than decorating.

You are easily bored by repetition and sameness, so you prefer environments that are stimulating. During the day when working or relaxing you may change rooms to create a sense of variety and increase your levels of stimulation, or get into a new way of thinking.

Equal mix of agree and disagree

You are somewhat open and somewhat traditional. Ideally your home should reflect this. You have a medium response to change. I suggest you read both of the other descriptive paragraphs and pick out the elements that reflect you the most. For example, you may not like to change décor often, yet you may have an extensive collection of vintage crockery!

Each of the big five factors can be split into different facets, so you will need to pull out what aspects of change and variety are the most relevant for you.

Mostly disagree

You are what is sometimes described as a traditionalist. You like 'tried and tested' ways to do things. Once you have established a good way of doing something, you stop thinking about it and you stick to it. You are less change-orientated than most people and don't see the point of making changes for changes sake. You like classical forms and styles and are less interested in new ideas and innovations.

You don't get easily bored by your environment. You like repetitions, routines and regular habits and you find the familiar comforting. In the home you will probably only decorate when the scheme looks tired and dirty, you have a leak, or you have peeling wallpaper. Once you've decorated and you're happy with your décor you may leave it just like that for many years. In fact, when you do redecorate, you might redecorate with a similar style and colour scheme. After all, why change it when you like it as it is? You will search for the shade of paint and the style of furnishings, the same or very similar to the originals. You may get frustrated when you cannot replace old things like for like because they have been discontinued.

You probably like traditional representational art rather than modern or abstract art. If you do like modern art it is likely to have some order, or a regularity to its form like geometry; truly organic and messy art does not appeal to you at all. If you like a particular artist you may display more than one picture from that artist on all the walls in one room because you like things to match and look co-ordinated.

How your openness to experience is expressed

Now you know your score on this trait you can compare it with your score on the introvert-extrovert scale. Psychologists describe openness to experience as a driver for cognitive exploration or, in other words, seeking new information to solve a problem, or seeking new sensory experiences and thrills. If you're an introvert then this driver

will be much more in your inner world, in your mind where you will be full of ideas. Whereas if you are extrovert your driver for exploration will be external and experiential like theatre, live music, and cultural experiences.

Personality summary

Common factors related to high scorers on openness to experience include: being imaginative; having a wide variety of interests; original thinking; being daring; a preference for variety; an aptitude for creativity and an attitude of curiosity.

Lower scorers are risk averse, dislike change, are practical, described as down to earth, and enjoy things that feel familiar including repeated experiences.

Knowing where you are on this scale will have a big impact on how you want to decorate your home.

Cabinet of curiosities. Before museums were created and funded by governments and philanthropists, wealthy members of society, who enjoyed collecting antiquities and exotic or rare objects, created cabinets

Lola's floral master bathroom. Lola is a maximalist artist. Her Instagram account shows her love of colour, pattern, and beautiful or interesting things. In her bathroom her collection of floral silk robes and vintage floral pics results in a much softer and romantic look when compared with most bathrooms.

or rooms to display these precious items they could proudly show them to friends and visitors. Eventually this trend led to creating museums, so that more people were able to enjoy the collections.

Design tips for the highly open to experience personality

- Embrace your love of the new, the curious, and the unusual. Display precious items that you have collected for your own pleasure, as well as to show to friends and visitors. These can be dotted around your home or clustered together on shelves, cabinet tops, or in special curiosities cabinets.

- Move things around from time to time so that you will see them with fresh eyes.

- Don't be afraid to occasionally have a clear out of objects if you need to make space for new ideas and things. However, don't feel the need to follow the minimalist trends. You won't like the result because the style doesn't suit you!

- Don't be embarrassed by your desire to constantly change; it's okay to be you. All personality types are equally valid. Do what suits you.

- Play with layout changes in your spaces and rearrange art and objects to change your views.

- Change your aspects of your home on a regular basis; it isn't just about the visual though, make sure you change smells, sounds, and textures too.

- Consider renting items rather than buying them, or buy cheaper second-hand goods if you like changing things around a lot. You can make money back by selling items you no longer wish to keep so that someone else can enjoy them.

Design tips for the more traditional

- Ignore trends and the feeling that you should want to change things. You know what style you like. It's ok to stick with it. It's your home and it suits you well as it is.

- Shop in traditional stores and antique shops, auctions, and markets. You will find quality items to suit your taste.

- Surround yourself with familiar things.

- Match your colour schemes and fabrics on items such as furniture, curtains, and cushions.

- Avoid change unless it's necessary. For example, moving house is stressful for you more than most; only do it when absolutely necessary. And only decorate when things start to look shabby.

Exercise

Write up your quiz results and any additional notes in your summary sheet in chapter 2.

- What answers did you find?

- Where are you on this trait? High, medium or low?

- What has this meant for environments that you've enjoyed spending time in, and environments where you have really felt uncomfortable?

- What design thoughts or ideas did the chapter or quiz raise?

Designer bias

Have you ever consulted a designer to help you in your home? Surprisingly, I have a word of caution for you here. Please pick your designer carefully. Look for someone who really cares about you and what you like and want. Someone with a good level of empathy and customer service who won't impose their taste on you.

I love creatives! As a designer I love to spend time with quirky and original designers, makers, and artists. We share ideas and inspiration and spark off each other. Ours is a world full of new ideas and, as a result, often out of pace with normal, everyday, 'average' opinions. Research has shown that many designers prefer bolder and louder colours and designs when compared to the general population. We tend to value items that are one off, bold, and unique. Many artists, textile designers, vintage hunters and up-cyclers fall in this group too. Not surprisingly in my experience,

creatives tend to have a higher score on 'Openness to Experience'.

So, if you have a low score on openness to experience, you may find some designers approaches are too over the top for you. One of the themes of this book is to find, and then follow, your own style. When designing for someone it's really important to create a space for them, for the brief, and not for the designer's own personal preferences. This is especially important when designing a home space. After all, it is the client who will live there day to day, not the designer. This may seem an obvious point, but the desire to design something fabulous that the designer will be proud of, is difficult if there is a clash in opinion or taste. To reduce this risk, look at their portfolio before you engage them. Find one that has done work that you like. Sometimes, the client can get swept along with new project enthusiasm, only to feel let down and

Becca is a colour loving maximalist. She painted these colourful stripes using masking tape of different widths and multiple paint colours to achieve this effect.

unsatisfied later when they realise that their new scheme doesn't suit them.

My advice here also counts for articles and magazines. These are full of lovely ideas and trends and lists of cool or exciting things to buy. Trends are based on opinions, and opinions are just that though, opinions. There is no right and wrong. Following trends can be a great way to find inspiration, but, please, don't fall into the trap of comparing yourself to other people and finding your taste or your home wanting. Many popular TV and magazine designers sell their ideas and preferences as the 'right way,' and I have read and overheard phrases like 'life is too short to be boring', or 'ban the beige', or 'move over magnolia' many times. As well as this, some designers, and especially those with a stylist background, or a shop where they sell accessories, will encourage you to 'finish' your design to a 'desired' level of detail of accessories, ornaments and art. This is great for a magazine shoot, a show home, or even a shared office. However, I strongly disagree with this approach in a home. Styling your home ideally takes time. Your home should be all about you and a reflection of your tastes, experiences and relationships. I really like the approach where homes are layered and built over the years. And of course this can apply to you if you have lived in the same home for a long time, but it can also apply when you have moved regularly because your objects of interest and treasured items will come with you.

Where you score matters

In the short personality trait quizzes so far you will have scored high, middle or low. And I'd like to make a comment on that now that you have completed three. When we score in the middle of the scale and don't have a strong preference, it is easier to see and appreciate differences in others. However, when we notice someone's tastes and preferences are very different to ours, this feels more dramatic and can lead to negative judgement.

When we enter the home of someone very different in personality to us, our sense of feeling at home is disrupted and we will feel much less comfortable. We may even feel on edge.

A stronger negative opinion usually occurs because we have scored very high or very low on a trait. Try to suspend your judgement and see the opposite of your preference as different, rather than wrong or without good taste. This is especially important when people with opposite personality traits share a home. And I give some tips on how to do this harmoniously in Chapter 15 – Considering couples.

Chapter summary

In this chapter we explored the third personality trait of the Big Five, openness to experience. We learned that when it comes to our environments, people who score high on openness to experience prefer novelty, variety, creativity and are curious. This is especially true when people score high on extraversion as well.

People who score at a lower level on the openness to experience trait prefer stability, habits, what's tried and tested, known and classical styles.

We also learned that the design industry tends to have a higher level of openness to experience. Don't let this influence you unless you want it to. If you prefer more traditional interiors and don't want to decorate every year then that is perfectly valid too.

Chapter 6

Agreeableness.
The warm and friendly trait

Is this the perfect host?

My Grandma Peggy was a lovely woman, a talented cook and a fabulous host! She rarely had a bad word to say about anyone, was full of great wisdom and advice, and always had soup or a hot drink and a hug to offer. She loved having visitors and worked hard to ensure all the family got along harmoniously. She would have scored very high on the personality trait called agreeableness.

Contrast this with someone who never or rarely invited you over; they prefer to meet people out and about, rather

A small selection of the author's extensive glassware collection

than at their house. When you do visit them at their home it can be a bit awkward. They might not offer you a drink or food because it doesn't occur to them. The comforts in their home have been set up for them, not guests. Don't make the mistake of thinking that they are ashamed of their home though; they probably do love their home as much as anyone, perhaps more.

Do you have a friend you love to visit? They have drinks on tap, a comfortable vibe, there's always great convivial company, and no tension. Physical elements make up the look of such a space but it's also about the atmosphere. Therefore 'agreeableness' manifested into a space is as much about the feeling the elements create, as a particular look or style. The physical features might include: squashy comfortable cushions or nice glasses to

drink from; a comfortable light level that is geared to the planned activity such as a bright light to play bridge or dimmed lights to watch a film.

An agreeable home is tidy and clean but not so tidy you worry about spoiling anything, and the way the furniture is arranged makes for easy conversation. Also, there are lots of little touches designed to make you feel almost as at home as you do in your own home; clean guest towels in the bathroom, multiple places to put your drink down, pleasant smells, relaxing sounds (not too loud, or quiet). In an agreeable person's home you don't worry about where to sit, you don't worry about whether you'll be taking someone's favourite chair. You know that you are welcome to sit wherever you want.

Agreeable people have a desire for harmonious relationships, and when creating spaces this translates into physical and emotional comfort, for themselves and for others. They may not be consciously aware of it, but they naturally put a lot of effort into this. For them it would be very odd not to.

Deliberately austere

An art gallery is a good example of a space that is designed with a deliberate opposition to creating seated comfort or an atmosphere that encourages lingering. The gallery has a specific purpose. The focus is on the walls. There are few or no seats. Any seats are designed for those looking at art and not for conversation. They are usually hard and would be uncomfortable to sit on for a long amount of time, so people don't overstay. The whole space is designed to show off the art but not in such comfortable surroundings to encourage too much lingering.

Fast food restaurants are neither agreeable nor like an art gallery. They fall somewhere in the middle. Often decorated in bright, fully-saturated warm colours (reds, oranges, and yellows) and bright lighting is deliberately placed to make you feel hungrier and welcome you in. But bright lights and hard surfaces in tables and seating also mean that once your appetite is satisfied, you move on quickly, which allows room for the next hungry customer.

Trait definition

People who score high on agreeability are warm, sensitive, empathetic, tactful and caring. They care about others and what others think, desiring harmony and, above all, lack of conflict. The extent to which they value positive relationships and harmony is key to their nature. Not surprisingly, this kind and considerate nature arouses trust and liking in others.

Art gallery

An agreeable person is easy to have a good relationship with, and they usually both make and keep friends easily. They are sensitive and empathetic to others. This requires no conscious effort. Like all personality traits, it comes naturally. An agreeable person will think hard before giving harsh feedback or rejecting someone.

The low scoring opposite is less agreeable and is not as concerned about maintaining harmonious relationships. Someone who scores low on this trait will tend to put themselves first, be known for being honest and expressing their opinion. Some may think this honesty makes them insensitive to people's feelings. Although they are likely to enjoy debates and arguments, this does not mean that they are aggressive and hostile. A person who scores lower on agreeability will also have lots of friends and positive relationships.

We've talked about the extrovert's home being built for socialising. Is agreeableness the same? At first glance it may seem so. But there are more subtle clues to look out for. Whereas an extrovert's home may be designed for gregariousness, largesse and showing off, the agreeable home will be designed to foster harmony, intimacy and psychological safety. Psychological safety occurs where people feel comfortable to express their thoughts and feelings without fear of judgement or criticism. And depending on the homeowner's level of introversion or extroversion, this home may be designed to host smaller intimate groups or large gatherings.

Although the feeling created by the host's welcome is as important as the design, here are some more design elements you may find in an agreeable person's home:

- Welcoming entrance areas, hallways and porches. Plenty of space for visitor's coats and shoes. A great first sign that this home may have many visitor comforts.

- Décor is not too bright or too homogenous. A happy middle ground is likely. One that will appeal to the vast majority of visitors at some level.

- People can easily see each other in the space and chat. They have enough personal space but are also all close enough to talk.

- The space is tidy and clean enough but not too much. Items strewn around give a relaxed feel, e.g. magazines and books left on the coffee table. A throw or comforter left in such a way that inspires confidence in the person that wants to pick it up and use it.

- Furniture is practical, comfortable and appealing. It is organised in a way that aids harmony.

- Temperature is carefully kept at between 19 and 21 degrees. This is the optimum comfort zone for the majority of people.

- Music is neither rousing nor soothing, and it's at a medium to low volume. It will fall in the 'easy listening' category.

- Food and drink are readily available, and items to facilitate this level of hospitality will be evident, e.g. cocktail bars or trolleys, drinks cabinets, breakfast bars, serving hatches, coffee tables, places to put down drinks, coasters, etc.

My aim in all these descriptions is not to judge others well or harshly or encourage you to judge others. Yet again this is a trait where society in general, values one end of the continuum above the other. Try not to be swayed by this; instead, I want you to really understand yourself, and what you are doing within your home. I want you to understand

A historical view of the interior of the House of Commons, central London

your own needs so well, that your home is built around you.

Should you aim to be a more agreeable person? No, please don't! You are you. There is no point in trying to make yourself more agreeable, unless that exists within you naturally. When we try to behave in a way that is not true to ourselves, it usually creates more stress. The home you choose to create is up to you, and for you. People who host, usually really enjoy it, and that's why they do it. If your home is a private space and a sanctuary for you that is perfect, please carry on doing that.

Space design, culture, and communication

After the bombing of the Palace of Westminster in London, UK, in May 1941, there was an opportunity to redesign the building and interiors. British politics has a long tradition of a two-party adversarial system. Although there was some discussion and suggestions for change at the time, Winston Churchill was adamant that he wanted the space rebuilt in exactly the same way, where the party in power and the main opposition party members sit opposite each other in the chamber. This is a great example of a space designed to suit the people who score lower on the traits of agreeability, because the seating style encourages debate. It was also built with the same number of seats, even though the number of MPs had grown over the centuries. There are still significantly fewer seats than MPs in the House today. A sense of urgency is created on important debating and voting days as MPs literally have to cram into the chamber. And this is what Churchill desired. He understood how the design and long-held culture of British parliamentary democracy were intertwined and famously said, "We shape our buildings and afterwards our buildings shape us."

Quiz time!

Are you intrigued? And wondering where you fit on this one? From the above descriptions you may have an idea already. You know the routine by now. Let's do a quiz to help you to see yourself clearly. Answer the following questions fairly quickly. Try not to think about your answer for too long. As always we'll analyse the answers at the end.

Please read the following statements and mark whether you agree or disagree:

1   I work well with others.

2   When making a decision, I try to take everyone's views into account.

3   When someone upsets or annoys me, I don't forget it easily.

4   I enjoy thinking about buying presents for people, wondering what they will like.

5   I always try to see the other person's point of view.

6   I sense it when someone is unhappy and try to be of help.

7   People tell me I'm co-operative.

8   I am an easy-going and care-free person.

9   I don't like it when people get angry with each other.

10   don't like to hurt people's feelings, so I keep critical thoughts to myself.

Your results!

Mostly agree

You are a friendly and relaxed individual who endeavours to make yourself and others feel at their ease as much as possible. You aim for a calm and harmonious home life, and you are likely to have set up your home to achieve this. For example, your furniture is more likely to be organised in a way to put people at their ease, which helps them to relax and easily communicate. When you act as host, you make more effort than the average person, to make people feel very comfortable and relaxed.

Equal mix of agree and disagree

You are in the middle range on this trait which means that you are neither agreeable nor less agreeable. Please read both of the other descriptive paragraphs and pick out the elements that reflect you, your behaviours, and your needs.

Mostly disagree

You are seen by others as someone who values telling the truth more than keeping the peace. For you, arguing is a healthy and enjoyable activity, and you see no problem with it. You do not go out of your way to make others comfortable anywhere, including in your home, because you see that as their responsibility. If they need something they will ask for it? You view your home as a place for yourself and your family. When people visit you in your home, you need them to adapt to you and your lifestyle preferences. You may prefer to meet people outside of your home so that you can relax and enjoy their company rather than having to think of their needs.

Personality summary

To summarise this trait, people scoring high on agreeability are: easy to live with, sensitive and empathetic to others, desire harmony, like spending time with people, and avoid conflict and hostility. Whereas those that score lower on agreeability are able to say what they think, may be good negotiators, and they tend to focus on tasks rather than people.

Design tips for the highly agreeable

- Create a home that enables you to host well and feel comfortable when you are doing so. Set out your furniture in an open layout which is known as centrifugal. People can see each other easily and at a comfortable angle and distance.

- Create places for people to be both sociable and solitary in comfort (extroverts and introverts).

- Do nothing in extreme – not too messy or tidy, not too colourful or bland, not too cluttered, or bare. Hit the middle ground in décor to keep everyone happy.

- Make sure you consider your own needs as well as those of others.

Design tips for the less agreeable

- Accept and celebrate the fact that your home is built around you and not others. Enjoy it guilt free. You may feel like your home is a sanctuary just for you and that's great! Not everyone needs to host. You can really create a space just for you to enjoy.

- If you do decide to host events at home, think about what people will want. It may not be the same as what you prefer. It might be a good idea to find someone more experienced at hosting than you and ask them for help to plan the event.

Exercise

Write up your quiz results and any additional notes in your summary sheet in chapter 2.

- What answers did you find?

- Where you are on this trait? High, medium or low?

- What has this meant for environments that you've enjoyed spending time in and environments where you have really felt uncomfortable?

- What design thoughts or ideas did the chapter or quiz raise?

Pretty evening party tablescape

This cosy space is perfect for solo time

Chapter summary

In this chapter we explored the fourth personality trait of the Big Five, agreeability. We learned that, environmentally, people who score high on agreeableness prioritise harmony, friendliness, calmness, serenity, and make interiors decisions based around the comfort and happiness of themselves and others. Whereas people who score lower on the trait of agreeableness are more prepared to say what they think, can cope better with conflict, and usually place the truth above harmony. Their interiors are likely to be mostly or entirely geared to their own preferences and needs.

We're really getting somewhere now in building a picture of you in your ideal home, and understanding how the different traits within the Big Five model interact to create your unique personality. We have also started to discuss some of the biases that exist within society which, unfortunately, put pressure on people to do things they think they should do rather than what they really want to do. Hopefully, you now feel that increasing your self-awareness and developing a deeper understanding of your personality and preferences gives you more confidence to resist such peer pressure.

Let's now move on to the last of the Big Five.

Chapter 7

Neuroticism.
The emotional stability trait

Are you sensitive to feedback? Or do you think that other people's opinions are none of your business? Your answers to these two questions will probably reveal your level of mood stability, or what is known as neuroticism.

Neuroticism is the last of the Big Five personality traits in OCEAN. But what does it really mean? Like the term personality, neuroticism has a popularist definition and one which psychologists use. In popular media and everyday conversation, the term neurotic is often used in a derogatory way, unfortunately. This is a real shame because, when used in the way psychologists define it, there is more nuance; it has both positive and negative aspects, and, as with all of the other traits, there are no rights or wrongs in how we are, just consequences in how we live. Although a high level of neuroticism does have its downsides, so does having little or no neuroticism at all. I wonder if that surprises you.

In recognition of the social stigma of the word and in order to aid the flow of this chapter, I am going to replace the word neuroticism with the friendlier terms of sensitivity and emotional stability. I feel that the softer words will be more helpful for you to consider the trait while we talk about it in relation to our environment.

Personality trait definition

Emotional stability is the extent to which someone feels they can cope with day-to-day life and its challenges. The higher emotional responses to circumstances include anger, anxiety, self-consciousness, irritability, emotional instability, and depressed mood.

People who score high on this scale tend to be more self-critical than most, more anxious, prone to worry, moody, emotionally sensitive, easily upset and also tend to be more thoughtful, analytical ,and reflective. If something bad happens in a day, a more sensitive personality will think about it a lot, whereas a more emotionally resilient personality will shrug any negative feelings off quickly.

People who score low on this trait tend to be calm, have little or no worry or anxiety, are less affected by the behaviour of others, shrug off criticism, aren't sensitive to conflict, and spend little time reflecting on things.

It's easy to see how a high score might be debilitating but can you now see how too low a score can also have unwanted consequences? So, there's lots to consider here for everyday work and living your life. But what does this trait have to do with interior design?

The five-factor model of personality is designed to capture the entire personality. I have included neuroticism here for completeness. Of the five personality traits discussed thus far, this has the least obvious impact on interiors, but it does have an impact, and I think you will be interested to understand how. Also, I have included some tips, especially for those that score

highly on this trait that I think people will find helpful.

An individual's level of emotional stability is not just about how sensitive someone is to other people. And it's not just about the response to another's moods, opinions, or behaviours. It can also be about the level of response to physical surroundings, such as lighting, sound, and temperature. When the weather changes, some people can physically feel the shift in atmospheric pressure. Also, some people have a heightened sensitivity to loud music, hot or colder temperatures, and strong smells. This is a really interesting area and we will cover an individual's responses to sensory input in more depth, when we talk about senses in Chapter 9.

Using feeling regulators or emotional snacks to self soothe

In Sam Goslings book 'Snoop', he and his colleagues describe students' dorm rooms and deduce the personality characteristics of the inhabitants from the way they have furnished, decorated, and styled their spaces. The kind of things they looked at were art and music posters, type of bed linen, photographs, candles, incense, cuddly toys, music collections, overflowing bins, clothes neat or strewn on the floor, beds made or unmade, keepsakes, colour use, textures of clothes/flooring/throws, and books and magazines. That's quite a list!

Student room

When the team are looking for clues in the dorms from all these items, Sam says that the personality trait neuroticism (or as we are thinking of it – sensitivity) is trickier to pin down and spot when 'snooping' when compared to other traits. One piece of evidence they look for he calls 'emotional snacking'. Emotional snacking is something that is especially important for people who have lower mood stability.

Sam noticed during his research that people use objects as 'feeling regulators'. What does he mean by this? An object used as a feeling regulator might be a picture of a loved one, or a situation that reminds them of a fun experience. It might be placed so they can view it often, or it might be in a private space like a drawer or the inside of a cupboard. This image reminds them of who they are and who they are connected to, which provides a comforting emotional moment. He describes the use of such items as an emotional or social snack. In the same way you might eat a chocolate bar for an energy pick me up, or look at a view of an image to positively impact mood.

So, a student, while seeking motivation during late night revision, might have a poster of a favourite celebrity or spiritual guru near their study area and glance up to view and 'snack' on them at key moments of study. Imagine a poster with the words, 'You got this!' or a poster that includes a poem that you find inspirational. And it's not just photographs or inspirational posters. The list of items that could be used to emotionally snack on is potentially endless.

Psychologists have described such items as a surrogate for the real attachment. This suggests that the way we decorate our environment creates a temporary emotional attachment to the space itself. For those of you with more knowledge of psychology, you will probably have noticed a link here with Winnicott's Theory on Transitional Objects where young children use objects as both a comfort and an assist to their development of a clear sense of self.

As a young person, at home and at college or University, all of your identity and belongings tend to be in one room: your bedroom. And, because of this, your sense of identity, with so many objects to view, is clear and often intensified during what, is for many people, a formative time.

Of course, the idea of emotional snacking does not just apply to student dorms. It is relevant for all homes and everyone. The difference being that items are distributed across an entire home and the items are not just visual ones. There are also plenty of examples of auditory, olfactory, and kinaesthetic items that someone might choose to have in their home environment to help them feel a feeling. A favourite bear might soothe you to look at it, feel soft when you cuddle it, and still have a familiar smell. Music has been shown to be emotively powerful. Playing music can both induce and reinforce feelings. For example, smooth jazz tends to be soothing, whereas heavy rock is stimulating. We all know a song that makes us want to dance, or a song we

Affirmation pebble

An old printers tray is the perfect space to display little treasures.

put on when we want to feel sad feelings. When we hear bad news, sometimes we want to tune into those emotions and music helps us to do that.

What feelings do you think objects can invoke or reinforce? Well, the answer is almost any feeling including: love, melancholy, safety, inspiration, anger, romance, creativity, relaxation, being energised, calm, hunger, or ambition. Experiencing and snacking on images and objects can cause a positive or negative change of state and feeling. The point is that it is the desired mood reinforcer or shifter that the person requires in the moment.

An unusual work motivation statement?

Quiz time!

You may have an idea already where you fit on this personality trait but let's see, shall we? Answer the following questions fairly quickly. Try not to think about your answer for too long. As usual, we'll analyse the answers at the end.

Please read through the following statements and mark whether you agree or disagree.

1　My mood can vary from day to day.

2　People can be really annoying.

3　It's easy to irritate and upset me.

4　I usually get nervous about new things.

5　It's easy to get disappointed when you are let down by someone.

6　I can get pretty stressed under pressure.

7　It takes a while for me to feel able to trust someone new.

8　I do tend to worry about things.

9　I can be happy in the morning and really sad by lunchtime.

10　I don't like to be challenged.

Your results!

Mostly agree

You tend to worry and feel unsure and have anxious feelings more than most people. This can lead to an increase in negative thoughts, overthinking, and subsequent low mood at times. Having a home that feels safe and secure is particularly important to you. You're likely to surround yourself with items and reminders of positive experiences that feel comforting and reassuring to all your five senses.

Your home will be full of soft and warm textures, clean and fresh smells; quiet spaces where there are no sounds or just soft music.

You are more likely to put up posters with affirmative statements or art that has meaning to you, such as a painting of a favourite beach or landscape. You will keep photos of loved ones nearby, as reminders of close relationships and use sentimental objects often: a favourite cup or gift or souvenir of a happy holiday.

You care about having things that make you feel safe and secure in your possession and you like to surround yourself with them.

Equal mix of agree and disagree

You are in the middle range on this trait which means that you are neither overly anxious nor emotionally stable. Please read through both of the other descriptive paragraphs and pick out the elements that reflect you, your behaviours, and your needs.

Mostly disagree

What is the opposite of a sensitive nature? The words stable and unruffled sum it up. You appear calmer and steadier than most people, and the majority of situations have no impact on your mood or self-esteem. Your home will probably have an absence of sentimental objects. You may see the ornaments and sentimental objects in other people's homes as pointless clutter. And if you are also low on the agreeability trait you will have no problem pointing that out to people!

Design tips for sensitive types

- Use objects at home and work that will enhance your feelings of stability and equilibrium.

- Take care with things that change daily, like scents and music. For example, rose is an essential oil that has been shown to reduce anxiety, and uplifting music or sounds of nature like bird song or water also have a restorative effect on mood.

- Take care of your body temperature. In cold climates, a comforting blanket or hot water bottle will soothe the body, which then soothes the mind. Alternatively, in hotter climates use ways to keep cool.

- Make sure your home is full of things that feel good to touch, like sumptuous cushions, wool throws, high quality bed linen, and soft fluffy towels.

- Put up lots of items that are visually pleasing for you: art and posters, affirmative statements, favourite art, photos of loved ones and sentimental gifts and ornaments.

- Protect yourself from things that will negatively affect your mood in the home. Things like a photograph of someone you have fallen out with.

- If you get anxious about safety in the home you might want to install an alarm system to reassure you.

- Use colours in your décor that you find soothing. These tend to be lower in saturation, for example, pastels and neutrals. More on this in Chapter 10.

- Layout your furniture away from the door, so that you can relax and enjoy what you are doing in the moment without thinking whether someone might come in. This is especially important in your bedroom.

Design tips for emotionally stable types

- You may see many ornaments and sentimental objects as frivolous and pointless. They may have no meaning to you, but it will enhance your relationship with others to appreciate that they are important to the people in your life that you care about.

- Although you are a resilient person, and most of the time there will be less interest in environmental concerns, there will be occasions when you feel more vulnerable and upset, so it's worth taking a look at the tips above. We are all emotional beings. You may find some of these tips useful too.

Dispelling stereotypes

In my teenage years, at school and university, the more sensitive teenagers always seemed to become goths. Despite being friends with them I never subscribed to the fashion; it just wasn't me. It was a fashion statement but also a stereotype. I think it's important to recognise that although high sensitivity might lead someone to design a gothic interior, it also might equally lead them to like a very white and clean interior, or a cluttered and colourful rustic and textured space. One answer on the personality profile will not give you enough information to assume everything about a person's taste. I find it reassuring that we are all so very complex. Try not to jump to conclusions about yourself or other people when it comes to personality or interiors!

Exercise

Write up your quiz results, and any additional notes in your summary sheet in chapter 2.

- What answers did you find?

- Where are you on this trait? High, medium or low?

- What has this revealed for you? Think about any environments that you've enjoyed spending time in and environments where you have really felt uncomfortable? Is there a link?

- What design thoughts or ideas did the chapter or quiz raise?

Emotional Sensitivity Summary

In this chapter, we explored the last personality trait of the Big Five, emotional sensitivity. We learned that on, an environmental level, people who score high on this trait tend to worry, feel unsure, experience more anxiety, think a lot of negative thoughts, and experience low mood at times. Having a predictable and reliable homelife and more control over their environment creates higher feelings of safety and security.

Whereas people who score lower on this trait are more emotionally stable, unruffled, and calm. For them, circumstances and events are quickly forgotten (whether positive or negative) and, as a result, they have little or no impact on the individual's mood or self-esteem.

Although feeling emotionally rocked can be difficult, the good news is there are lots of things that can be used in our environment to soothe us.

A reflection on all five personality traits in conjunction.

This is probably a good time to look at your scores on all the Big Five and think about the interactions between each of your personality scores, and what that means for subsequent taste in your home environment.

For example imagine a person with a high score in conscientiousness: they are also introverted, have a low score in agreeability, and are highly sensitive. This person will most likely want to create a home that is quiet, very organised and really easy to clean. It has no clutter, but it does have clean lines and lots of storage. Guests are rarely invited. It's just for them! Can you imagine a person like this and their ideal space?

Let's try another example. Imagine a person who has high sensitivity, and high agreeability combined with introversion and low conscientiousness. Here I see a very relaxed and textured home. There are rugs, cushions and throws to snuggle under. Nice smells and soft music waft through the space. Lots of pictures of loved ones and favourite holiday snaps on the walls. The homeowner likes to invite individuals or small groups of friends round for cosy chats and intimate dinners. Can you imagine this person and space?

So there are two quite different home examples! Do you have anything in common with either of the examples above? What is your summary so far? How would you describe your home and what do you think of it in relation to you? Does it reflect you well? Might you change to make it fit you better? Hopefully, you are starting to see what

works and doesn't work well for you in your home and why. We will come on to guide you in making changes to your home in Chapter 14, when we pull everything you've learned together.

A note on minimalism and maximalism

In some quarters much is made of whether it's best to be a minimalist or a maximalist in interior design. A minimalist interior can be described as one where there is a limited and muted colour palette, very few objects, clean lines, clear surfaces, and definitely no clutter. Added to this visual description is a calm atmosphere, a quietness or low level of music, and there are few rough textures; everything is smooth and low-key, including lack of scent. In contrast, a maximalist interior is one that gives the viewer a 'full-on' sensory experience with lots of colour, pattern, textures, objects of interest, and objects on the wall; there might be loud, vibrant fast paced music, chatter, olfactory evidence of cooking activity, and many textures and materials to come across.

Quite often the debate between the two is divisive or binary. You may have been told that you should be one or the other. Hopefully by now you will have realised it depends on you and what you are like! If you put these two trends on a continuum you would

The green room at Ham House
(National Trust)

find the maximalists end occupied by homes with lots of bright colour, patterns, objects, busyness and noise. These homeowners are likely to score high in extraversion and openness to experience; whereas the minimalist camp with homes defined by clean lines, muted colours, and no clutter will be occupied by the highly conscientious and introverted personality types. And, somewhere in the middle of these two extremes, you will find the rest of us!

Temporary changes in personality can be due to stress or illness.

As an adult our personality scores tend to be fairly fixed from one year to the next. For example, we don't spend one year being mainly introvert, followed by another year being very extrovert in our behaviour and preferences. However, sometimes our personality can shift. Major life experiences, too much stress, or an illness can impact us in many ways, including our personality. This change might be temporary or permanent.

Here are a couple of examples to demonstrate this point.

An individual who has been through my 'Discover your Design Personality' process, got in touch because she had a desire to make her home in the UK more colourful during the first Covid lockdown, which was late spring 2020. This was an unusual request and took me by surprise Normally she has a preference for a neutral palette, and she doesn't like bright colours at all. She was surprised too!

As we discussed some options, I realised why her design desires had dramatically changed. During the first Covid lockdown, everybody's mobility was limited, and people who normally got lots of brain stimulus from being out and about, were now dependent on their home environment for all their needs. Normally, someone who scores highly on the introvert scale finds everyday life very stimulating and sometimes overwhelming, so they often use their home as a haven to return to and relax in after a busy day. A neutral decor and minimalist interior helpfully soothe an over-stimulated mind. But in the first few months of dealing with Covid many people couldn't go out. So that meant that all of our stimulus had to be generated from family, phone calls, our homes and garden.

In terms of interiors, my advice to her was to add in changes gradually, with pops of colour in layers, and in movable objects like pictures, cushions, throws and rugs. This way, she could more easily undo things when the lockdown had finished and her life returned to its usual busyness. Many months later, she thanked me from preventing her for making overly dramatic decorating decisions. As I suspected, when life became more free and she was out and about again, her desire to decorate and change her home went away.

Here's another example from an opposite perspective. I was approached by someone who is a brilliant therapist and healer. She asked my advice about a client she was treating who was absent from work due to stress. Her client was normally an outgoing and extroverted personality. Her house was full of objects and books that normally gave her pleasure. However, whilst ill she felt stressed and her environment at home had become claustrophobic. She wanted to have a major declutter and remove a lot of her stuff. I explained to the healer how our personality is linked to our environment and that, because her client was feeling more vulnerable and spending more time at home, the vibrant and stimulating environment which she usually loved was too much for her to take in because she was unwell. This view had not occurred to the healer because she was a much more introverted personality, and was leaning on the idea that it was a good approach to de-clutter and create a minimalist setting to assist this lady in her healing. My advice to the healer was to help her client to remove some objects, but store them safely. Then, when her client had fully recovered, she could sort through her possessions, decide what she wanted to keep, and what she still wanted to dispose of.

Chapter 8

Mood

So far we have explored five traits of personality. Traits are aspects of self that are fairly fixed. What could be the opposite of that? What can shift in a moment? The answer is our mood.

What does the word mood mean to you? The Collins dictionary defines mood as follows: "Mood can be both a noun or adjective, singular (one person) or collective, e.g. "I'm in the mood", or "He's in a funny mood", or "The mood of the people". In the context of interiors and this book, think of mood as the temporary emotion someone feels at any given time. We will explore the way a space either evokes or deepens a mood. Mood is the absolute opposite of personality because our environment can change it.

By its very nature mood has the potential to be much more malleable. However, we do like to form habits and patterns of behaviour, and this impacts our mood. People have moods they choose, moods they prefer to feel, and emotional states they put effort into creating. In fact, human beings have a lot more control over how they feel than they sometimes realise, and the environments we create and choose can really help with this. If you think of an environment like a busy pop concert and compare it to a morning lie-in under the duvet, or a blustery coastal walk compared with a quiet moment spend in a vaulted cathedral, you will conjure up very different emotional responses to those places and spaces.

So, we can evoke the moods that we want to feel, when we choose to, by being more conscious and choosing our environments carefully, or changing the environment we are in. For example we can dim or brighten lights, open windows, light a fragrant candle, put on music

Opposite page: inside the Sagrada Familia

or TV, pick up a cosy throw and settle into a comfortable settee. All of these examples can conjure a variety of feelings. The difference between watching a funny film or sad film to access a desired emotion is probably obvious to most people, but a scent or piece of music can also dramatically change mood in an instant. This effect is further amplified if it is charged with a memory of a place, person, or situation. More on using memories in design in Chapter 13.

Why is mood so important in Interior Design?

One of the first and really key design questions to ask yourself when designing a space is, 'How do you want to feel here?' Considering the desired mood of a space is often where professional interior designers start their design process because a well-designed environment clearly and easily evokes a desired feeling. I've chosen two very different environments here to explain this point.

The first is the incredible Sagrada Familia in Barcelona. Designed by Gaudi, construction started in 1882, and is still ongoing at the time of writing. As a result many generations of workers' hands are in this building. All cathedral architecture is designed to inspire the awe of God within humanity and this one is truly phenomenal. Outside, the spires reach to the heavens. The enormous, cavernous, vaulted interiors are beyond a scale that we are used to on a daily basis. Sun streams through the huge stained-glass windows and everyone is bathed in luminous coloured light. The combination of the beauty, towering

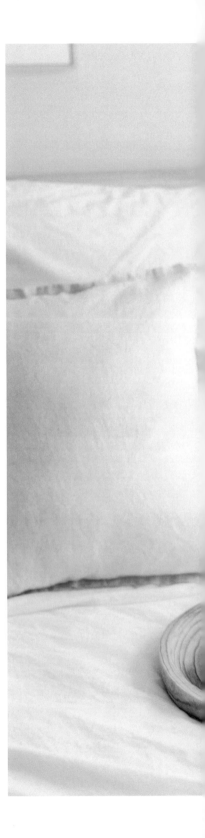

stone columns, stained glass, endless marble floors, and intricate wood and stone carvings combine to create a wonderful experience, and an inevitable deeper emotional and spiritual response. The many human visitors seem tiny, despite their numbers, and their hushed voices create an atmosphere like nothing else.

Sunday lie-in, breakfast in bed

I've deliberately chosen a scenario that is as opposite to the first that you can imagine. This one is cosy, private, intimate, and, one of home. Imagine a lazy Sunday morning. You wake up and stretch in comfort, smelling fresh, clean sheets. It's wintertime and you can hear the wind blow as rain splashes noisily on your windows. Someone is making breakfast. Coffee scents mingled with orange juice waft towards your nose; the Danish pastries and hot toast and butter are warm and delicious. You are free to decide what you're going to do with your day. Nobody needs anything from you. You are comfortable, safe, and cosy in your homely nest.

So, there we have a start, with two very different experiences. These spaces are at either ends of the spectrum with so many other mood-inspiring space experiences in between.

Quiz time!

As with the previous chapters it's now time for a quiz. This one is really simple to do. We all experience many emotions, but it also makes sense that you will have some preferred states of being, so let's explore.

This next section is designed to be illuminating and works best when done quickly. Don't think too hard about your answers. Be instinctive if you can.

Instructions: Look at the table above and consider the words. Which five appeal to you the most? Not just in terms of home design or fashion. Circle the words that appeal to you the most in life.

Some questions

How did you find this exercise? Was it easy? Or did you want to do more than five? Please try to limit the number so you can easily analyse it.

Circle the five emotion or mood words below that appeal to you the most:

Passionate	Calm	Sophisticated		Melancholy	Energised
Joyful	Thoughtful	Sensitive	Enthusiastic	Playful	Chilled
Safe	Contemplative	Silly	Meditative	Muted	Cheerful
Creative	Stimulating	Sad	Expressive	Seductive	Sociable
Relaxed	Optimistic	Communicative		Comfortable	Serious

Did you find it hard to circle five? The list is not meant to be exhaustive. If one is missing that is important to you, please write it in.

Once you have circled five words, we can move on to analysis.

Analysis

1 Of the words that you have circled, how much energy do you think they have? For example, if you have circled 'quiet', 'sad' and 'calm,' they are all lower energy words. The words 'enthusiastic' and 'cheerful' have higher energy. Have you chosen high, medium, or low energy words? Or a mix?

2 Of the words that you have circled, now consider how positive, neutral or negative they are. For example, if you have circled 'cheerful', 'safe', and 'optimistic' these are all positive words, whereas if you have circled 'melancholy' and 'sad' these are negative emotions. There are many more words here that are more neutral and neither positive nor negative; for example, 'calm', 'thoughtful' and 'contemplative'. What combination do you have?

3 Are there any themes to your words? Themes might be social, light-hearted, uplifting or thoughtful. Are your words similar to each other or do you have a lot of contrast? Is there a pattern emerging or is it more eclectic?

4 Now, once you have decided on your words, have a look back at your Big 5 scores. Can you see a link or multiple links to your scores here? For example, you might have scored very low on

the extrovert trait and chosen calm and quiet. Or you might have scored highly on the sensitivity trait and chosen sensitive and safe.

The combination of words that you have chosen may reveal a sense of the proportion of types and styles of spaces needed in your home. If all of your words are similar, then the spaces in your home will be ideally decorated in a similar style. Whereas, if you have a mix of words, you might prefer to separate the spaces and decorate them differently. Or you could create the mix in one space: for example, one client I worked with chose 'quiet', 'calm', 'thoughtful', 'serene', and 'silly' as his preferred mood words. There is no way I would have known about his silly side if he hadn't told me in our session. He is mostly introverted. His silliness is a deeply held aspect of self that is mostly private and only shared with close friends. It's unlikely that he would have volunteered the information within a normal consultation. When designing for him, I made sure that there were small elements of silliness to add in pops of fun, in what was otherwise a very grown-up and sophisticated design.

Positive and negative feelings

People have a tendency to want to only focus on feeling positive and upbeat. But sometimes we don't feel good. There are many valid reasons for a low mood. I encourage you to embrace all of your moods. We all need to let ourselves feel serious or sad feelings sometimes. For example, if we have experienced a bereavement, a disappointment, a loss, or, a betrayal, then it's really good for us to express the feelings that naturally follow. Rather than fight negative emotions, you can use your environment to support you. For example, if you are feeling sad you might surround yourself with comforts and warmth, or if you are angry you may play music that reflects and expresses the rage. You may not want to create a room in your home that reflects sadness or rage all the time, but you could create a space that you can rearrange and change to support you at the appropriate time.

Moody designs

Now you have an idea about what emotions or moods you want to evoke in your home, we can start to explore how interior design can help you to achieve this. There are some classic design principles and tricks that designers use to help achieve a particular mood. The way they use colour, patterns, lighting, layouts, hard and soft materials, styling, special objects, symbolic objects, art, repeats of forms and shapes. All combine to create the desired effect. At this stage in the book I will show you four

Vibrant, colourful and energising space

examples of moods created by light and colour use. I won't go into too much depth of explanation though, as we have more personality areas to explore yet.

The first two interiors are brightly light, colourful and very busy. There is a lot to look at. Look at the colourful glass chandelier! The overall feel is a high-mood energy which is cheerful, light-hearted, bold and playful. In Big Five personality terms, this space suits someone with medium to high extraversion and high openness to experience scores.

Sunrise, the yellow sky echoes the bright yellow lampshade

The images overleaf are examples of much calmer spaces. In both settings the colours are very dark yet inviting. The combination of the room colours and the dimmed lighting is flattering. There is much less to look at when compared to the brighter images, yet the rooms have texture, interest and style.

I wonder what you thought of each image. Whether or not they appeal to you will be linked to your answers so far in this process. Interior design can be quite intimidating and baffling as a subject because of the wide variety of scheme options available to create the same mood. Be reassured that we are on a journey to pare down the options.

You are well on the way to defining a style and approach to suit you.

What mood do people want and where?

Most of our homes are laid out in a similar fashion: we have hallways, bedrooms, lounges, kitchens and kitchen diners, bathrooms and sometimes offices and/or playrooms. I tend to find a lot of commonality between the emotions and moods people attribute to each room in the house. Here are some 'mood' ideas for you for each space. Which words feel most fitting for you?

1   Hallways: inviting, welcoming, open, friendly, private, exclusive.

2   The living room: family space, cosy, comfortable, relaxing, safe, fun, social, private.

3   The kitchen: organised, clean, abundant, family, friends, sociable, energised.

4   The bedroom: quiet, calm, romantic, comfortable, relaxed, private.

5   The bathroom: rejuvenation, relaxation.

6   The home office: organised, efficient, creative, professional, casual, fun.

These two dark schemes create a calming mood.

Creating the moods you want

This isn't it for mood. It's just an introduction. We have touched on how to create a mood with examples above and there are many elements that combine to complete a successful space design. These include: colour, lighting (both natural and artificial), materials use (both hard and soft), imagery, art, objects, flooring, styles, space, layout, paint effects, textures, fabrics, patterns.

As we continue to build the picture of your personality and interior preferences the elements that will conjure the designs you desire will automatically include what moods you want to create. Please try to hold this in your mind as you continue to work through the exercises.

Your Design Personality at Home

Exercise

Now you have completed this section on mood it's time to fill in the summary sheet in chapter 2. You may also want to make some notes around the following questions:

- What do your mood words tell you that you need in your home space(s) and other spaces that you spend a lot of time in?

- If you share your space what do you think your family or friends that you share with need?

- Are you starting to think about changes you could make in your home to suit you? What are they? Make a note of them.

- Do you have the proportions of high and low energy, or happy and sad moods right in your home or space? If not, what would you change first?

- What would your ideal home look like in terms of space design and space use? And what about getting the right mix of moods in spaces?

- What other thoughts or ideas did the chapter or quiz raise? Write it all down on your summary.

Chapter summary

Understanding how to design a space in order to create a mood is fundamental to good design. In this chapter we have explored what kind of moods you prefer to feel and what types of interiors you like to spend time in. Moods are changeable and are the opposite of personality which is mainly fixed. We have a lot more control of mood then we think.

Hopefully, you now have a good idea of what emotional states you like to be in, and what proportion of time you like to spend in each of them. Understanding how different elements like colour and light evoke mood is a key foundation in interior design. Exploring the possibilities of mood and space starts to give you a lot more insight to how your environment impacts your life.

Chapter 9

Senses and perception

It's Saturday night and you're going out to dinner. Imagine yourself walking into your favourite restaurant. What do you see around you? What's the décor like, the art, and the layout and pattern of seating arrangements? Can you identify the style they have gone for, and do you think they have got the lighting right? Is the overall feel more comfortable or elegant? Hopefully, you are greeted by a friendly face, and there are delicious smells coming from the kitchen. These are some of the many different sensory aspects of space available to you in one moment!

Klosterhaus, Bristol

Sensory lighting

Klosterhaus is a beautiful European-style all-day 'Grand Café'. The lofty space, open feel, classic furniture, sumptuous materials of velvet, gold, and glass, art deco shapes and classic lighting all come together to create a modern experience with a nostalgic feel.

Often, people talk about design as if it were a purely visual phenomenon. And that makes an odd kind of logic because, in order for us to operate well on a day-to-day basis, our brain limits what we consciously pay attention to. In our daily environment there is so much stimulus for us to take in, we could not consciously evaluate each individual thing in each

moment. There are literally millions of details we can sense, and, if we continued to sense them all, it would overwhelm us. So our brains simplify it down to a handful of items.

However, when designing a space, it's important to remember that we experience the world through our five senses: sight, sound, smell, touch, and taste. When designing we need to consciously think about each element separately, that, when combined, makes up how we respond to our environment. An excellent design considers all of the aspects of human experience and perception. And this is not just for those with sensory impairment. Paying attention to our sensory needs when designing space is important for all of us. Of course, once the design and refurbishment is finished, we can go back to just enjoying, and not thinking about why we like it.

In this chapter I will use the following terms to describe the five senses we experience the world through:

- Visual or by sight is what you see.

- Auditory or by sound is what you hear.

- Kinaesthetic or by feel is both what and how you feel (this is at least twofold; it can be what you feel like internally when you stroke a soft, woolly blanket, but can also be a sense or feeling of atmosphere like tension between people, or a sense on the skin from a thunderstorm).

- Olfactory, i.e. what you smell.

- Gustatory, i.e. what you taste.

Although the senses are separately identified, there is more crossover in sensory perception than you might think, in how we experience the world. For example, taste is influenced by what food looks like, smells like and even sounds like. Can you imagine celery without the crunch? Or lemon without the citrusy smell? Could you tell a lemon apart from a lime without the cue of the yellow rind? If you think, yes of course I could, then I challenge you to taste them whilst blindfold! You might be surprised. Did you

know that our level of thermal comfort, or how warm we are is influenced by colour and light? In experiments with a steady temperature, participants consistently report that blue rooms feel colder and red rooms warmer. In his book 'Sense', Russell Jones says, "Our senses constantly crossover, working together as one sense; profoundly influencing how we think, feel and behave".

Some people have a condition called synaesthesia. Synaesthesia is a neurological condition in which stimulation of one sensory or cognitive pathway crosses to stimulate another automatically. When one sense is activated, another unrelated sense is also activated. Imagine hearing music and simultaneously sensing the sound as swirls or patterns of colour. Linking seeing colour with hearing music is one example, but there are many variations of how this occurs, i.e. which senses are crossed and how they are crossed. It is thought around 3% of people experience this phenomenon. I suspect some people have no idea that they have this ability. They probably think everyone experiences the world the way they do, and this is an important point, I think. Do we experience our environment in the same way as others? Probably not. It is extremely unlikely that we do, but it's really hard to tell because our perceptual experiences are so personal to us.

Although synaesthesia is a fascinating condition, it is rare. For most of us, sensory input is linked but not crossed. What is interesting about each of us though, is that we have a unique way to use each of our senses. Have you ever wondered if you pay attention to one sensory input more than others? One way to find out is to explore the language you use every day. The language you use has been shown to reveal which senses are more influential or important to you.

We give out clues to this in what we say. For example: "Do you SEE what I mean?" "How do you FEEL about that?" "I like the SOUND of what you're saying", and so on. Isn't that amazing? You may know about this already through a topic called Neuro Linguistic Programming (NLP). In NLP theory the internal messaging which relates to our five senses is known as modality.

We will soon explore your sensory dominance with a quiz. Perhaps you're beginning to understand which sense you prioritise and prefer already. The preferred sense(s) that you filter through will impact your interpretation of experiences.

Senses and Design

In terms of interior design this is really important to know. For example, if someone has an auditory dominance, the quality of the sound management within a room will have a more significant impact on them. For example, when music is playing or there are lots of people talking, this individual will be more likely to feel really uncomfortable if space acoustics are not well managed. Below is a real example for you to explore.

In the paragraph below I've listed how you might perceive each element with a marker after each sentence. K for kinaesthetic, etc. For me, the most vivid sense in my imagination was the warmth of the sun and the breeze on my arms. I am highly kinaesthetic. What were your strongest sensations?

Imagine a day at the beach. It's warm and sunny. There's a strong smell of sea, salt, and sun cream. The sea sparkles in the sunlight. You can hear the waves crashing and the sound of children playing and squealing with happiness. The hot day creates a shimmer over the sand. The warm breeze slightly ruffles the hairs on your bare arms, and you love the feeling of the warm sunlight on your skin. A faint tinkle of an ice cream van sounds in the distance and immediately your taste buds come alive already imagining the taste of a vanilla 99 cone with a chocolate flake and raspberry sauce. You can see it dripping down over the cone.

Beach huts

Imagine a day at the beach. It's warm (K) and sunny. There's a strong smell of sea, salt, and sun cream (O/G). The sea sparkles in the sunlight (V). You can hear the waves crashing (A) and the sound of children playing (K & A) and squealing with happiness (A & K). The hot day creates a shimmer over the sand (V). The warm breeze (K & A) slightly ruffles the hairs on your bare arms (K), and you love the feeling of the warm sunlight on your skin (K). A faint tinkle of an ice cream van sounds (A) in the distance and immediately your taste buds come alive, already imagining the taste (O/G) of a vanilla 99 cone with chocolate flake and raspberry sauce. You can see it dripping down over the cone (V).

Quiz time!

From the above description you may have an idea already which sense or senses are more important to you. Let's explore a few examples with yet another quiz! More questions to help you understand yourself and how you experience the world.

Have a read through the following scenarios and then close your eyes and imagine your experience of them. Think about which sensory element is strongest for you. Sometimes you may have more than one.

The answer grid and score sheet is on the side. For each scenario you have 10 points. Allocate your points according to how important the sensory factors are.

What is your dominant sense?

Sensory scenario	Sensory score (out of 10)
You're sitting quietly in a cinema watching the trailers. The sound is booming out of the speakers. You look up at the giant screen at the colourful and engaging advertising trailers. You have been anticipating this film's release and are excited for it to start! Your partner leans across to whisper something to you. You can tell they are excited too. The seats are comfortable and covered in soft velour. The cinema is an old Art Deco place and you can just make out some of the features in the dim light, beautiful lights, velour seats and deep red velour curtains. The smell of popcorn and hot dogs wafts across you. Suddenly, it's time. The film is starting!	Visual Auditory Smell/Taste Kinaesthetic
It's a beautiful Spring day and you are walking in the countryside. The sky is blue and the air smells fresh and fragrant. There is a light cool breeze blowing, and the sun feels warm on your face for the first time in ages. As you walk on the path you hear your feet crunch on the gravel, and the birds and bees are buzzing. There is a beautiful carpet of blue, yellow and pink spring flowers.	Visual Auditory Smell/Taste Kinaesthetic
You haven't seen a good friend for ages. You are planning to meet up at her house. Imagine the greeting. What are the first things you think about experiencing? What will you notice first? What will you notice and enjoy the most?	Visual Auditory Smell/Taste Kinaesthetic

Sensory scenario	Sensory score (out of 10)
It's a lovely hot day at the beach and you've decided to go for a swim in the sea. At this end of the beach it's fairly quiet and there aren't many people around. The cliffs loom over you as you walk down awkwardly over the pebbles and rocks. You enjoy watching the sparkles of sunshine on the waves as they crash noisily to the shore. You anticipate that the water will be cold, and it is! Once you are in, though, that feeling of cold subsides, and you enjoy the feeling of the sea on your skin, and the smell of the salt water.	Visual Auditory Smell/Taste Kinaesthetic
You popped out to the shops and got caught by a Summer thunderstorm! It came out of nowhere. One minute it was sunny, then you heard a rumble, looked behind you, saw a looming black cloud, and were startled by a very loud clap of thunder! The next thing you know the raindrops are bouncing off the pavement, you are quickly wet through, and your thin t-shirt sticks to your skin. As you run home you feel the rain hitting your face, and you can taste the rain. The smell of the wet earth rises to meet you.	Visual Auditory Smell/Taste Kinaesthetic
You're at a party and are being introduced to a friend of a friend. As you lean forward and shake their hand, you automatically look them up and down noticing their smart attire, freshly showered and slightly curling damp hair, and surprisingly colourful shoes. You are greeted with a warm smile, good eye contact, and a friendly handshake. You appreciate the sparkly, vivid blue eyes that are returning your gaze. When they speak, about a recent holiday, their voice is slightly husky and steady.	Visual Auditory Smell/Taste Kinaesthetic

A young woman enjoys the storm from under her yellow umbrella and (above) a view of empty velvet red theatre seats.

Sensory scenario	Sensory score (out of 10)
You have decided to go to the museum on your day off. As you walk in you can smell cleaning products and mustiness. Despite the warm day outside, it's cold inside. There is no queue and the friendly smiling teller gets you a map of the building and exhibits. The sounds of people talking echoes around the large, vaulted foyer. You admire the architectural features and sympathetic colour scheme, and decide what to visit first.	Visual Auditory Smell/Taste Kinaesthetic
You're on holiday and you've decided to eat somewhere new. What factors are important to you? Imagine yourself looking in through the window, browsing through the menu (outside). What are you paying attention to? The décor is simple, light, and fresh. It's about half full of people and there's a low level of chatter. People are smiling and laughing and there's a friendly vibe. The aromas coming from the kitchen are garlic and herbs, fresh bread, and a sweet note you can't quite identify.	Visual Auditory Smell/Taste Kinaesthetic
You are discussing going to a music gig with a friend. The same artist is playing at a large venue and a few smaller more intimate venues too. You think about what your experience might be like at both. You are only going to book one of them. Which would you choose and why? How do your sensory preferences impact your choice?	Visual Auditory Smell/Taste Kinaesthetic
Recall a recent pleasant experience. A special day out. Close your eyes and transport yourself back to that time. Describe your day to yourself in your mind. What are you experiencing? What sensory elements stand out to you the most?	Visual Auditory Smell/Taste Kinaesthetic

Scenario	Visual	Auditory	Taste/Smell	Kinaesthetic
Cinema				
Spring day				
Good friend				
Beach				
Thunderstorm				
Party				
Museum				
Holiday eats				
Music gig				
Pleasant day out				
Totals				

So, how did you fare? Did you get the result you expected or were there some surprises? Many people I take through this exercise are surprised by the result. They assume they will be mostly visual. Did you?

To help you understand this exercise a little more I'll share the results of when I did this exercise. As you can see from the answers below, I am aware of all five senses in most scenarios. Kinaesthetic is by far the most important area for me to pay attention to when designing for myself, but that doesn't mean the other areas aren't important too. In fact, the other three factors are closer together by score than the first and second senses. It's important to pay attention to all senses when designing. This exercise shows me that comfort, textures, and a relaxed atmosphere are top of my list. What's top of yours? What did you find out from this exercise?

Scenario	Visual	Auditory	Taste/Smell	Kinaesthetic
Cinema	2	4	1	3
Spring day	2	2	3	3
Good friend	1	3	1	5
Beach	2	2	3	3
Thunderstorm	2	2	1	5
Party	2	2	3	3
Museum	5	2	1	2
Holiday eats	1	3	2	4
Music gig	1	3	0	6
Pleasant day out	2	2	1	5
Totals	20	25	16	39

Circle your dominant sense(s) and then have a think about what that means in terms of designing the ideal environment for yourself from a sensory point of view. If your dominant sense(s) is/are:

Visual - This means that the first thing you notice is visual. The colours, patterns, etc. It's the overall look that will dictate how you feel in a space.

Auditory - Quality of sound is important to you. You hear the different levels of pitch, loudness, and timbre. Your acoustic experience will dominate how you feel in a space.

Smell/Taste - The most emotional and primeval of senses. Good smells will instantly improve mood. Bad smells motivate us to get rid of the problem! Your olfactory experience will dominate how you feel in a space.

Kinaesthetic Textures, feel of materials, temperatures, and atmospheres (emotional) will be the first thing you notice in a room. Your kinaesthetic experience will dominate how you feel in a space.

As with other aspects of personality and individual differences, there is no one particular sense that it is better to be dominant in. All are valid and unique. The next time you're talking to someone, pay attention to the language that people use. We reveal quite a lot about our sensory preferences with conversations like:

Person one: "Urgh can you smell that?"
Person two: "No. what smell?"

Or

Person one: "OMG! the sound of the drills outside are really getting to me."
Person 2: "Oh really? That's a shame. I haven't really noticed. I've kind of blocked it out."

Here are some design tips for each sensory perspective.

Knowing where someone's sensory dominance lies when you are designing a space helps direct attention to all the right places.

In his book 'Sense' Russell Jones suggests creating a positive sensory coming-home ritual that will reinforce your 'feeling of home' and clearly end the working day. Simple things like popping the kettle on, lighting a scented candle, or changing into comfy clothes will help you to relax. These rituals are even more significant and important for us if we work from home all or some of the time.

Here are some tips for designing interiors where one sense dominates. You may want to read through all of them though. The tips in here may be helpful even if you aren't especially dominant in that sense.

Design tips for those with visual dominance

Your needs are the most straightforward to meet, as your brain, the design industry, and society in general, is very visually cued already. Magazines and sites like Instagram and Pinterest are full of glorious images designed to fill you with inspiration and ideas. To meet your visual dominance needs, pay particular attention to colour use and combinations of colour, geometric and organic patterns, the quality of natural light, and use of artificial light, when designing your space. Of course you also need to keep in mind your other preferences discovered so far, the Big Five personality and mood.

So, if you have a high score on Extroversion or Openness to Experience, you will want lots of bold or mid-hued splashes of visual interest in décor, art and objects like fresh flowers and colourful cushions. If you have a high score on both traits, treble that thought! More is more in your case! Whereas, if you have a lower or low score on extroversion and are more introverted or you scored lower on openness to experience, you will want calmer, neutral or more subdued colours, less pattern and fewer objects. Of course you can be a mix i.e. high openness and introversion or low openness and extroversion. In which case it's worth taking time to decide just what level of visual stimuli feels right for you. Whether you want high or low impact, do take time to getting colour schemes exactly right. Whatever your Big Five scores, if you are visually dominant you may see or notice subtle variations in colours more than others. We will talk about colour and how to choose the right palette for you much more in chapter 10.

Getting the lighting right in both daytime and evening will be especially important to you. There is a world to explore with lighting options around lux levels and light colours. Think about your lighting schemes and how they work at different times of day and in natural and artificial light. Consider that you will care more about coloured lights (from warm whites to cool blues) and light brightness levels. If you are extroverted you will like brighter lights or more options. People who are introverted and those who score lower on emotional stability will be more likely to prefer subtle and subdued lighting.

If you combine a visual sensory dominance with high conscientiousness, keeping surfaces clean and dust-free will be a priority for you. Choose materials that help achieve an easy clean. Place books and ornaments in glass-fronted cabinets to reduce dust and don't have open shelves in a kitchen which can be a nightmare for collecting a combination of grease and dust.

If a room has an odd and imbalanced layout like oversized furniture or semi-blocked doorways, you may be more visually 'jarred' than most. If you also score high on conscientiousness, then creating visual symmetry in a space may be key for you to feel comfortable. Do you find yourself straightening rugs and pictures? If so I suggest you pin that rug down with a rug gripper and keep pictures straight with mount squares.

Exercise

These are just some of the many ideas out there. Pull out your summary sheet from chapter 2. You may also want to make some notes around the following questions:

- Which of these ideas appeal to you?

- What do you think matters to you most as a visually dominant person?

- What does having this sensory dominance tell you that you need in your home space(s) and other spaces that you spend a lot of time in?

- What easy thing could you change in your home now that would meet this need?

- What other thoughts or ideas did this section raise? Write it all down on your summary.

This light-filled space is neutrally decorated and ideal for someone who desires peace and quiet. Furniture is sparse and there is a solitary chair which hints at the desire to be alone. Materials are rustic and natural.

The perfect room for someone who is high in sensitivity and kinaesthesia is a space full of privacy and comfort. This sumptuous hotel room at Heath Hollow Hideaway has lovely materials and feels luxurious, cosy and very, very intimate.

Design tips for those with auditory dominance

Sound and sound scapes impact us all. Everyone is sensitive to noise at some level. As babies, we are born with only two instinctive fears, falling and loud noises. Your answers suggest that understanding the sound management and acoustics in a space is more important to you than anything else design wise. Sound travels in waves. When it meets a soft surface like a curtain, carpet or cushion, it is absorbed or muffled. When a sound wave meets a hard surface like a wall, ceramic floor or windowpane, it bounces and continues to the next surface or ear drum. The scale, surfaces, materials, furniture, equipment

and layout in a space all affect the way sound travels and impact what is known as 'sound quality'.

The current trend of pared back interiors has lots of hard surfaces and this can make a space very noisy if no management of sound is considered. For example, many restaurant owners make the mistake of not considering sound when refurbishing their space. This can lead to an unpleasantly noisy experience for customers on busy days, when there are lots of diners. The noise of other diners talking travels and the sound reverberates in each person's chest area; not conducive to enjoying the meal or good digestion. Those with auditory dominance will feel the impact of this poor sound management more than most.

The key to creating a space that is 'just right' sound-wise is to balance the amount of soft and hard surfaces. Too much soft covering will result in a muffled soundscape which can feel a little weird. Don't worry too much about this though, as it's unlikely that you create this situation. It's more likely that you won't absorb enough sound and you will need to add more soft surfaces.

I meet people who say they are not interested in interiors, then, if I change the subject to that of music systems and sound, they will suddenly become engaged! Because you care about sound quality, you may be an expert in where to place speakers within a room to create the perfect listening experience. Maybe you haven't considered this to be an aspect of interior design until now?

You are likely to be easily disturbed by unwanted sounds at home and work. My advice is to choose both environments carefully. If you are choosing where you live, consider the environment around the property. Are there businesses like pubs or restaurants locally? If so, you will experience more noise than residence-only streets. The era of when the property was designed and built is also worth considering. For example if you live in an old cottage with very thick walls you will have a different experience of hearing your neighbours when compared to living in a home built in the last 50 years.

You are less likely to enjoy open-plan living because of potential noise pollution from family, spouse or friends. Multiple noise experiences such as the TV on in the lounge and the radio on in the kitchen will annoy you! Although open plan is popular with many families, it makes good sense to keep some walls and doors within your house so

that different family members can enjoy separate activities without disturbing each other. And if you are buying your appliances such as washing machines, dishwashers and fridges, you might want to consider spending a little extra to reduce the decibel level generated by these appliances.

There are two types of sound to consider. Within the space and beyond the space. For example, if you are converting a building into two flats you'll come across building regulations developed to ensure that there is adequate sound proofing in the floor area. This subject becomes quite technical, and adding more information is beyond the scope of this book, but I encourage you to look into it if you are considering having building work done at home. In a domestic setting where you wish to reduce noise within a property, you have a number of options to help you achieve this. The first is flooring. Hard floors such as tiles, wood and concrete will increase sound, whereas softer flooring like carpet and rugs will help to muffle sound. Other items in your home

Sound proofing solutions for home

like curtains, soft furniture, cushions, throws, tapestries and plants will absorb sound. Even wooden panelling will disrupt the way sound moves through a space. In commercial settings sound baffling can be employed in ceilings and walls. If you desire a minimalist aesthetic with quiet soundscape then you might consider installing these in your home too. Acoustic panels can be fixed to walls and ceilings and integrated or hidden in a way that suit your style. Here are some great examples of wood panelling that not only look fabulous, but also absorb sound.

Sound management is a specialist area and worth researching in depth or engaging with an expert to help create the perfect sound experience when it's important to you.

One last thought for you about good noise management in your home, is to think about which activities you do, where, ideally, you have more peace and quiet. For example, if the back of your house is quiet but at the front of your house you can hear noise traffic, then you might choose to do sociable activities at the front of your house and quieter activities like reading or watching TV at the back. There is no rule book that I know of, that says where you have to do different activities in your home. Some people happily live in 'upside down' houses where the bedrooms are at the bottom and the lounge and kitchen are at the top. This can work really well for a number of reasons like noise management, or making the most of a view.

Exercise

These are just some of the many ideas out there. Pull out your summary sheet from chapter 2. You may also want to make some notes around the following questions;

- Which of these ideas appeal to you?

- What do you think matters to you as an auditory dominant person?

- What does having this sensory dominance tell you that you need in your home space(s) and other spaces that you spend a lot of time in?

- What easy thing could you change in your home now that would meet this need?

- What other thoughts or ideas did this section raise? Write it all down on your summary.

Design tips for those with gustatory/olfactory dominance

This is an unusual sense to have as a dominant one, and for those that do, I usually find that they are very aware of it because it has a big impact on their day-to-day living. Our response to smell is very instinctive; the majority of people don't consciously think about it, but we do immediately respond to it. The primitive part of our brain, the amygdala, developed first (before the prefrontal lobe) and it has an immediate response to negative or positive tastes and smells. If it's a good smell then our instincts tell us, 'That's great, let's have more of it, let's stay here, I feel safe.' But, if it's a bad smell like rotten food or drains, the response is, 'Let's get rid of it, let's get out of here, this is not safe!' Our sense of smell is a critical part of our survival instinct.

For those that have this dominant sense, things like the smell of bad drains, lingering smells of cooking, new paint or carpet, cleaning products, and wet dogs can ruin your day! Here are some ideas to help you get your interior design right if this is your dominant sense.

My first piece of advice is relevant for everybody, but it really applies to you. Have you ever noticed a new car smell? Or the smell of paint when you have just finished painting a room, or the smell of a new mattress? It's really important to know your VOCs in new products,

including, fresh paint, flooring and furniture. VOC stands for volatile organic compounds, and are chemicals that have a high volatility of molecules in the surrounding air. VOCs are responsible for the odour of scents and perfumes as well as pollutants. Some VOCs are harmless and some can be dangerous to humans and the environment. When you bring any object into your home you are also potentially bringing in polluting chemicals. Examples of VOCs that are found in everyday products that are toxic at high levels are: benzene, formaldehyde, chloride, toluene, and xylene. That's a pretty potent cocktail of chemicals. Although the majority of VOCs dissipate into the air quickly (a process known as off-gassing) some VOCs continue to off-gas for years. So it is worth finding out what pollutants you are potentially bringing into your home for the sake of your health and those you live with.

These days many residential and commercial paint companies advertise low, or no VOC levels. It's easy to check on the label. It's also easy to check the materials and manufacturing processes (including items like glue) for furniture and carpets with the supplier before you buy. One of the smelliest new purchases at home is new wood floors, vinyls or carpets. Sadly, we can't always assume that natural is better.

Natural products like wood are low VOC but might emit them because of the

Mel's loo has leopard wallpaper and pink paneling. What a great way to add bright colours, fun and interest to a small space. Perfect for the design personality with high scores in extroversion and openness to experience!

glue used in a product, whereas synthetic fibres like nylon can be low VOC. In general, hard floors like wood, stone and tile have the lowest VOC levels, and vinyl and carpets contain VOC in the dye, fibres, glues and backing. Natural fibres tend to be better than synthetic, but it all depends on the whole fitting process and materials used there too. Now you know about VOCs, think about what you want to check out before you buy. It's so annoying when the joy of a new floor or mattress or sofa is diminished because it smells terrible! Second-hand furniture is a good bet if you are sensitive to smells as any off-gassing will have

been completed long ago. I realise that will feel really counter intuitive to many people! Some old furniture has been better made than new if it's been well looked after too. One clue to quality in wooden furniture is dovetail joints. But I digress.

Continuing on the theme of chemicals, do you know what is in your cleaning products? Or plug-in air fresheners? As a person with an enhanced sense of smell please do check the ingredients in your home cleaning products. It is just as easy and effective to use natural materials to clean. These include lemon juice, vinegar and bicarbonate of soda. If you don't want to do this you can buy off-the-shelf products that are made from less harmful chemicals. Generally, if the product is less harmful to you, it's also less harmful to the environment, especially aquatic life, streams, rivers and seas. That's got to be a bonus, hasn't it? And, if you like a pleasant smell like vanilla in your home, or floral or citrus, it is safer to use essential oils (in tiny amounts) which have been distilled from plants and flowers, rather than chemically produced fragrances.

In the days before most homes had central heating, it was common practise for home-owners and housekeepers to regularly open windows and let fresh air into the home in all seasons. This makes sense when you consider the VOCs we've just talked about. And it's a practice I encourage you to do regularly, all year round.

In areas that are prone to mould, for example, kitchens and bathrooms, allowing fresh air in to circulate through the home is especially important. Because of bathrooms smells and shower steam, bathrooms need good ventilation, so, in today's modern bathroom, a powerful extractor fan is a must have. Sometimes bathrooms don't have big windows and some have no windows at all; extraction in such cases is critical to avoid condensation, damp and mould.

Kitchen smells can dominate a home long after the meal has been consumed.

So, you may wish to avoid open-plan living, and keep your kitchen separate. It is popular in some countries to have two kitchens: a wet kitchen and a dry kitchen. The wet kitchen is the more functional kitchen used for any frying or steamy cooking, and has easy to clean commercial features like tiled walls and floors, powerful ventilation, big work surfaces, deeper sinks and huge fridges. The dry kitchen is the aesthetically pleasing version, a space to be with family and guests. It's equipped with counters to serve from, and sinks and small fridges. The dry kitchen design is focused around serving up food and drinks and hosting. Many dry kitchens have bar space for stools or chairs, whereas in the wet kitchen all the real work is done. Once you've created the food, it can be brought through to guests. If you can afford this, it's a great way to reduce smells and still be sociable in a kitchen diner space. Otherwise, again, a good quality extractor fan is essential.

Plants and fresh flowers in the home and workspace have been shown in research to offer mood improvement and health benefits. We are hard-wired to be appreciative of nature and plants, and flowers add a soft, natural visual and olfactory aesthetic. But did you know that plants also remove pollutants from the atmosphere? Those very VOCs that we might want to get rid of, like formaldehyde and benzene. And plants have been shown to have healing and restorative qualities in healthcare environments. Research has even shown an improvement in performance in work environments where plants are introduced. How amazing!!

Whether or not you are likely to clean regularly, a cleaning routine will reduce smells and dust in your home. Also surfaces and material choices such as leather settees, ceramic-tiled floors and hard window treatments will help you easily keep a cleaner aesthetic. The problem is you might not like those material choices. So, if you enjoy a maximalist interior with lots of soft furnishings, then you might want to consider ways to ensure you have a regular and thorough cleaning routine? Even if it involves paying or getting someone else to do it for you.

A strong sense of smell can be a problem when you're out and about. A solution is to use essential oil support when on the move and when you are not in control of

Essential oils are a safer and healthy way to improve your home's fragrance

your environment. Carry essential oils - roll-on or spray - with you to use on your hands and wrists when going out. This tip helps me to cope better with unpleasant smells in some situations. You might also want to take a cleaning spray for things like airplane/train seats and trays.

It's important to mention that the olfactorily sensory world is a sophisticated one. Smells aren't just good or bad, and some scents have a powerful impact on mood. A smell can change how we work and how we think. Essential oils are natural but that doesn't mean they aren't powerful. Using essential oils in the home or workplace has been shown to influence behaviour. For example, research has shown that peppermint will increase productivity in mundane tasks, lavender can help relaxation and sleep, and rose reduces stress levels and anxiety. If you are interested in finding out more about this, many reputable essential oil producers have formulated blends of oils that are designed to create different desired moods and there are many useful books on the subject. Some of these books are included in the reference section at the end of the book. I have got into a routine of burning an orange essential candle while writing this book. The fresh citrus scents are uplifting and help me focus. And the regular habit of writing is reinforced by the smell. For other tasks I switch the scent.

Exercise

These are just some of the many ideas out there. Pull out your summary sheet from chapter 2. You may also want to make some notes around the following questions:

- Which of these ideas appeal to you?

- What do you think matters to you most as an olfactory/gustatory dominant person?

- What does having this sensory dominance tell you that you need in your home space(s) and other spaces that you spend a lot of time in?

- What easy thing could you change in your home now that would meet this need?

- What other thoughts or ideas did this section raise? Write it all down on your summary.

A note about taste. You may have wondered why I have combined olfactory and gustatory in this section. In terms of interiors they are inextricably linked. Because we do not eat our interiors, the link to taste is accessed by smell, so I have chosen to focus on the two senses together.

Plants at home are great for healthy air, they look great and they even improve sound quality

Design tips for those with kinaesthetic dominance

There are three aspects of being kinaesthetic that are relevant to homes and spaces.

The first is physical. Things that you can touch, sit on, cuddle under, etc. Being more touch sensitive or tactile means that you pay more attention to the importance of materials and how things feel. All soft surfaces and furnishings are an obvious lead here, such as carpets, rugs, sofas, curtains and cushions.

But the feel of hard surfaces is important too. The choice of materials is a top priority for people with kinaesthetic dominance. When considering a new floor think about how you will choose it. Do you prefer wool or synthetics, a stone floor or a wooden one? What type of rug might you choose? Warm underfloor heating under stone or ceramic tile feels like an incredible luxury to some and vaguely pleasant to others. Choosing what kind of hard surfaces like kitchen cupboards and work surfaces are more important to you than others. Take your time in choosing expensive items like this and make sure you get real samples before you order, so you can touch them. The usual considerations for a kitchen work surface are budget, look and practicality. As a kinaesthetic person you need to add 'feel'. The feel of a space and the feel of the materials will be the most important factor for you in creating an ideal space. Don't let people persuade you that the look is more important when you know that for you it's the feel. Being kinaesthetic doesn't mean you necessarily want more warmth or texture. It means that whatever material you prefer you feel more strongly about.

Imagine a bedroom that is all white. White walls, floor, bed, linen, accessories, lighting and wardrobe. The bedroom I have described has the potential to be really bland and will need texture to break up and add variety to surfaces so that the whiteness does not all blend together.

The second aspect of being kinaesthetic is the visual cues or clues as to what a surface will feel like from objects and surfaces in a space. For example, is the material in that rug rough or smooth? Is it natural? How does the quality of light play on the surfaces in the space? Even if you are not touching the material, you have a good idea of how that material would feel, and that is more important to you than most.

The third kinaesthetic area is quite different from the first two and that is one of atmosphere. A question we all subconsciously ask ourselves when we enter a space is, "Do I feel comfortable here?" "Is it conducive to my mood?" This really strongly links to all the earlier personality questions about creating your ideal space. For example, if you have high agreeableness, then you will care how the textures in the space combine to create comfort and harmony.

Aspects of design that create the right atmospheres involves so much and we still have more topics to explore. When you are pulling all your ideas together to see how they work, using a mood board will help you to create the perfect atmosphere. I will go into much more detail about how to create and utilise mood boards in Chapter 16.

We all have an ideal space design for us and those who are kinaesthetic are more sensitive to atmosphere, and thus negatively impacted when spaces don't work for them, i.e. the opposite of what they would ideally choose. For example, if someone had a love of horror films and a collection of movie posters depicting their favourites could you stay in that space and be comfortable? Your answer will be a clue to your scores on neuroticism and kinaesthetic sensory dominance.

Exercise

These are just some of the many ideas out there. Pull out your summary sheet from chapter 2. You may also want to make some notes around the following questions;

- Which of these ideas appeal to you?

- What do you think matters to you most as a kinaesthetic dominant person?

- What does having this sensory dominance tell you that you need in your home space(s) and other spaces that you spend a lot of time in?

- What easy thing could you change in your home now that would meet this need?

- What other thoughts or ideas did this section raise? Write it all down on your summary.

Design tips for those with sensory limitations.

Multi-sensory design is a popular approach when designing for people with special needs in this area. Essentially, if a sense is physically absent or diminished then design can help to compensate. One way is to ramp up the intensity so that the individual can sense what's there. For example, to compensate for partial sight loss, special light sculptures and lighting installations can have a wonderful impact. Similarly, for people with hearing impairment special vibration enhancing equipment can be used. In all cases though, when designing a well-used space, it's important to add in flexibility and think of all users. An ideal space is one which is sensitive to everyone's needs and, if it's a public and mixed space, some users may need a calm space as an alternative, so they aren't overwhelmed by the extra stimulus.

Are you a Highly Sensitive Person?

What if you feel you are more sensitive than everyone else? Then you may

Neutrally decorated and boho-styled bedroom

be one of the 15% of people that are known as 'highly sensitive'. Elaine Aron's work as a Clinical Psychologist led her to research and develop her theories about highly sensitive people (HSP). She includes herself as an HSP too.

Elaine Aron conceived the concept of high sensitivity in 1991. HSP is a subset of what's known as SPS or Sensory Processing Sensitivity and people with it are thought to be more sensitive to their physical environment than the general population. HSPs (those with high levels of SPS) display increased emotional sensitivity and a stronger reaction to environmental stimuli like light and noise. This sensitivity may show up in a number of ways and through her writing and therapy Elaine helps HSPs to better understand and cope with being more sensitive. It's worth pointing out that being an HSP is different from introversion. Although more introverts are also HSP, some are not; some HSPs are extroverts.

What clues might you have that you are HSP? Do you really dislike loud noises, bright lights, fireworks and violence on TV? Do you sense tension and conflict in situations more quickly than others? Do these sensations lead to feelings of overwhelm at times and the need to retreat or hide away? Do you avoid situations where you know you are likely to be overwhelmed?

If some or all of these scenarios feel like they might be true, I highly recommend reading her book as it is full of explanations as well as tips for coping and adapting to your HSP nature.

So what does this mean for your home? When the outside world is so full of overwhelming stimuli, having control at home is so important. Valuing your home and creating a sanctuary either in part or all of your home where you can retreat when you feel overwhelmed is a relief. The kinds of things you can do when creating your own style of sanctuary will be in response to your sensory dominance and HSP. So, for example, if you are mostly auditory in the way you experience the world and HSP, then make sure that you have good quality music, radio and tv sound systems, and good sound insulation between rooms (walls and floors). You might also consider choosing to live in a quiet or at least quietish area.

There is still so much to discover.

I've talked about how art, architecture and design currently tends to be visually dominated. In addition, psychologists and neurologists have shown that the amount of brain processing required for visual perception is considerably greater than the amount of brain processing for other sensory perception.

So taking those two professional viewpoints we could conclude that vision does dominate. And that the more the brain works on something the more important it is? But how can we be sure? As the field of neuroarchitecture is increasing in popularity I am optimistic that there will be a corresponding increase in research which will include sensory design.

Interestingly there are collective cultural differences here too. Whilst in Western and industrialised societies sight and hearing are dominant, other cultures have been shown to prioritise smell and taste. When researchers studied twenty different languages around the world they didn't find a common hierarchy of sense between language groups and cultures. Those that spoke English had precise language to describe colour whereas other languages in countries such as Lao and Mexico had developed more words for describing taste. And in the Australian Aboriginal tribe Umpila the researchers found that their most precise language terms were prioritised for smell! If you want to find out more about this subject I recommend Matthew Cobb's book 'Smell: A very short introduction'. It is a fascinating read.

And of course, remember, we do not sense in isolation. Our experience is multisensory. Research has already shown there to be a number of interactions, such as the link between lighting colour and thermal comfort.

Some historical perspective relative to sensory environments

I suspect that most of you reading this book will have good access to clean running water, toilets and efficient sewerage systems, and cooling refrigerators that keep food safely edible. In the 21st century much of the developed world has incredible sanitation systems. Many take for granted the comfort of multiple indoor bathrooms and privacy when toileting. Yet just 2 or 3 generations back in the UK and Europe many families had an outside loo and a tin bath in the kitchen for a weekly scrub!

In Europe's industrial age, cities became more populated and more polluted and inevitably incredibly smelly. In 1858 the famous 'great stink of London' led to Parliament approving the build of a proper sewerage system, which is still in use today. Thomas Crapper improved the S bend into the U bend in 1880 but it was not widely used in many countries until well into the 20th century.

According to the World Health Organisation (in 2020), 54% of the global population (4.2 billion people) used a safely managed sanitation service, but over 1.7 billion people still do not have basic sanitation services, such as private toilets or latrines. Bad smells aren't just unpleasant. They are signals for diseases like Cholera, E coli, and Typhoid.

Exercise

Now you have completed this section on senses it's time to fill in the summary sheet in chapter 2. You may also want to make some notes around the following questions;

- What thoughts or ideas did the chapter or quiz raise? Write it down on your summary.

- What is your dominant sense(s)? Or do you have an evenly distributed sensory life?

- How does your dominance sense link with your other personality factors?

- Does the section on HSP, sensory impairment or synaesthesia impact you?

- What will you do with that information?

- Do you have any aha moments from reading this chapter?

Chapter summary

Sensory design is an important yet often overlooked aspect of interior design. We experience the world through our five senses and sometimes this experience overlaps. Understanding which of your sensory filters you prioritise will help you to create a space perfectly designed to meet your individual sensory needs as well as all the other personality needs you have discovered so far.

There's such a lot that lies underneath our normal awareness in sensory design.

You may wish to go through the exercises and read the tips more than once to discover all you need to know about yourself and those close to you with regard to this area. I think it's worth spending time developing a deeper understanding of your preferences. Building this awareness will mean that you will be able to direct your time and money on the things that will have the most positive impact for you when designing your personal spaces.

Small child seen exploring a sensory room. These rooms are designed especially for children with sensory impairment; the additional stimulus for all 5 senses is stimulating and enjoyable.

Chapter 10

Colour

Colour is a hugely powerful phenomenon in our visual world. Many of us take it for granted and we're used to seeing the full colour spectrum. But not everyone can see all colours; just watch a video of anyone who is colour blind in the moment when they are given glasses that improves their ability to see the world in all its colourful splendour and you will witness their strong emotional reaction when they get to see our wonderful world in full colour, for the first time.

When designing or decorating a space, it's common for people to start by talking about colour. It's everybody's first go to. By now, I have hopefully shown you that there's lots more to design and décor than just colour. I have left the subject until now in this book, because I tend to find that, once the subject of colour comes up, other parts of the discussion can be diminished or lost.

Colour is a fantastic and impactful element in design. So I'm excited to get to this point and be able to share what I know with you and help you develop your own individual relationship with colour.

Do you think that designers conjure magic when they create a scheme? They may be acting with instincts, but all designs can be analysed and a few principles are usually at play. You just need to know a little bit more information and you will have everything you need to create a perfect room scheme yourself.

A quick introduction on colour theory

There's so much to learn about colour choices and colour combinations. Let's start with a brief introduction to colour theory. I promise to try and make this brief and not too theoretical!

The way humans see all colours is a process dependent on light. Our eye receives signals in the form of wavelengths and our brain interprets this information, turning it into what we experience as sight. All organisms with sight have light receptors within the eye, which are called rods and cones. Humans have three types of cone cells which have different ranges of detection of the colour spectrum. When one of the cone cells isn't functioning it results in colour blindness in a particular colour range. About 8% of men and 1% of women have some form of colour impairment. This makes the world appear significantly different for them. They have the ability to differentiate between 10,000 and 100,000 different colour hues. That sounds like a lot but, when compared to most people's ability to differentiate over one million colour hues, we can start to understand the visual impact of being colour blind.

The full colour spectrum is shown below. At either end and beyond most human eye's capability are ultraviolet and infra-red.

Animals and insects also have sight, but we know that they see or perceive objects differently to us. When a bee approaches a flower, it sees an ultraviolet pattern that looks remarkably like a tiny runway signalling a welcome entry to the flower and leading the bee to the pollen on the flowers stamens. The bee sees colours that humans cannot see and flies right in!

VISIBLE SPECTRUM

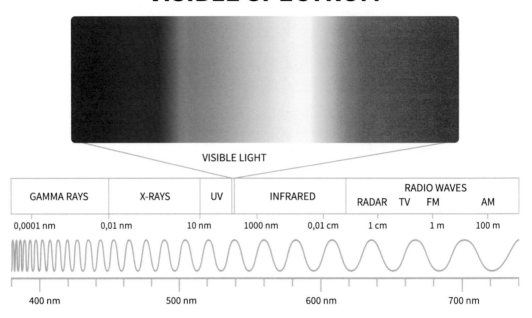

VISIBLE LIGHT

GAMMA RAYS	X-RAYS	UV	INFRARED	RADIO WAVES			
				RADAR	TV	FM	AM
0,0001 nm	0,01 nm	10 nm	1000 nm	0,01 cm	1 cm	1 m	100 m

400 nm   500 nm   600 nm   700 nm

Understanding the relationship between colour and light

Sir Isaac Newton retreated to the country to escape the bubonic plague that was sweeping through London in the 17th century. As part of his work and during a period of personal discoveries on many subjects, he investigated light refraction through prisms, named the spectrum of colours found in rainbows, and discovered that we perceive colour through light. Much of what is theoretically understood about light and colour today, is owed to, and based upon, Newton's discoveries.

The concept of the colour wheel was also invented by him at this time, when he joined the ends of the spectrum visible to humans, i.e. red and violet, and so bent the colour spectrum into a circle. There are many aspects of the way we use the colour wheel today that are really helpful for artists and designers. We will shortly look at the colour wheel in more detail, when we consider what colours go well together in room design. Newton said, "For in those days I was in the prime of my age for invention and minded Mathematics and Philosophy more then, than at any time since." We have a lot to thank him for!

Perception matters

Colour blindness is not the only way that colour perception varies between individuals. Because we (or our brains) interpret the light signals, the vibrancy of colours is also dependent on our physical capacity to perceive and this is affected by many things, including our mental state. Research has revealed that people who are depressed see colours less brightly or even grayscale (grey, black, and white). So when we say that people have 'the blues,' perhaps we should say more accurately that people have 'the greys'. Of course this also means that when we feel happy we really do see the world in full vibrant colour. The link between colour psychology, personality and mood starts with the way we perceive.

Colour psychology

Colour psychology is an incredibly popular topic and people are excited about its potential. So, what is it? Colour psychology research explores how people's experience of colour has the ability to change or influence their mood, behaviours, thoughts, and feelings.

The use of colour or exposure to different colours has been shown to influence people in a number of ways. These include increased feelings of competitiveness and aggression, and increased probability of winning in sport. In the field of romance and dating what we wear will impact how attractive we look to others. Room décor

A bee enjoying nectar from a foxglove

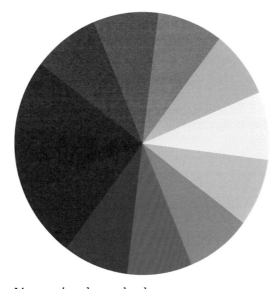

Newton's colour wheel

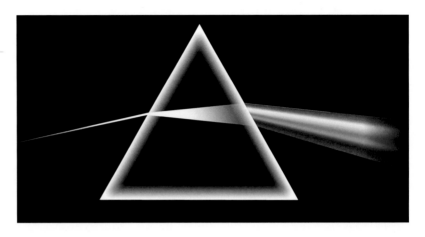

and everyday materials like plate or bowl colours can affect so much, including our perception of how warm and cold it is in a room, and how hungry or tired we feel. In workspaces the right colour décor can encourage creativity or intellectual performance. It's a really interesting field of knowledge.

To introduce the subject properly, I want to track back into our evolutionary past. We have two reactions to colour in our environment: instinctive and learned. Firstly, our instincts around colour are hard wired into us, and by that I mean we share them across all humanity. Secondly, our learned response is our own individual experience, but it is also influenced by the family, country and culture that we grew up with. This is nature and nurture; or genetics and socialisation at work and our response to colour is a combination of both.

Sometimes though, what we learn can feel very quick and instinctive, so we feel it is hard wired when it isn't. I want to help you to explore and understand your individual reaction to colour so you can use that

knowledge to your advantage when designing your home and workspaces. And you may find this insight helpful in other areas of your life too.

So now we have covered our instincts and individual experiences, we can add the further variables of context and colour hue. Colours mean different things to each of us, in different contexts. And there are many contexts to consider: relaxing, holidaying, playing sport, dating, eating, working, or evaluating danger. And for each main colour there are many variations of that colour or hue. The possibilities and number of variations in colour is huge. For example, let's look at yellow. As with all colour hues there are so many shades, tones and tints of yellow. You might find the yellow tone of someone's skin a worrying sign of jaundice, the yellow yolk of a fried egg for breakfast appealing, the pattern of the yellow and black stripe on a wasps jacket a warning and the bright yellow of a bunch of daffodils, cheering. That's four examples of yellow, four different contexts and four very different mood responses.

When it comes to interiors, the key to what we individually prefer in relation to our personality is based on the level of saturation, tint, tone or shade that exist across the colour spectrum, rather than just the colour itself. I probably need to explain my language use here. Level of saturation refers to the depth of the colour or hue; a tint is what the colour looks like when white has been added, a tone is what a colour looks like when grey has been added, and a shade is what a colour looks like when black has been added. For example, you may dislike a bright red but really like red when it's been mixed with some black to make wine red or burgundy. There are many different tints, tones and shades of colour hues as shown in the colour wheel below.

So to summarise, the reason our psychological response to colours or the colour psychology is so difficult to pin down is because we each have an individual difference in our response to colours, in terms of personality, cultural background and personal history. Also there are many different tones or level of saturation in each colour group; there are many colour groups; there are many different contexts in which we can experience colour; and we rarely see one colour alone; in fact, the way we perceive a colour is almost always altered by a colour neighbour.

Unfortunately, enthusiasm for the subject of colour psychology has led to some overly quick assumptions. There is much myth, misinformation and misunderstanding about colour and its impact on us. I have a great

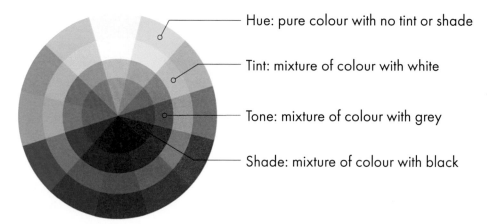

Hue: pure colour with no tint or shade

Tint: mixture of colour with white

Tone: mixture of colour with grey

Shade: mixture of colour with black

The differences between hue, tint, tone and shade

story for you which demonstrates why it's good to take commonly shared stories and information about colour and its impact, with a pinch of salt!

Perhaps you have heard of a colour called Baker Miller pink? In the 1970s a researcher worked with a naval correctional institute in the US, where they painted some prison confinement cells a particular colour and evaluated whether it would have a calming effect on prisoners. The colour was a vibrant pink and the colour was named after the two naval officers, Baker and Miller. It's a pretty striking colour which reminds me of bubble gum. They decorated the holding cells on board ship and they noticed that inmates were pacified and violent behaviour was reduced.

Much enthusiasm among researchers and beyond was felt at the time and the experiment has been quoted and shared in media and literature many times since. It's

often quoted to be scientifically proven and now belongs in our collective 'knowledge'. This is despite the fact that subsequent studies examining the influence of the colour Baker Miller pink on behaviour have yielded conflicting results. Some studies suggested that the calming effect was very short-lived and then there was an opposite effect and prisoners became more violent. In one experiment pink was compared to deep blue which is a different tone. So in that study it was not clear whether it was the colour or the tone that impacted behaviour. The fact that some people believe it is calming may influence their individual experience and it works for them, so it's story continues to be repeated. Add this to the idea that pink is soft and romantic and associated with weakness and femininity (in western cultures) and the myth is complete!

For a moment I'd like you to reflect on the colour pink. What do YOU think of it? There are many different pinks. Do you like some and not others? Let's take three examples: dusky pink has a brown undertone, fuchsia pink is very bold, baby pink has a lot of white in it and is soft and delicate. And that's just three pinks! So different, but all known as pink. Perhaps you like dusky pink, but you don't like baby pink. Or vica versa?

I don't have a firm opinion about pink, but I'd like to offer you an alternative view. Pink has the base of red; it's mixed with white to make pink. In colour psychology, the colour red has a strong evidence base. Red clothing has been shown to improve a woman's level of attractiveness and improve a team's likelihood of winning when worn as a team strip. Neither of these results is at all associated with being gentle or calm? So why is pink so associated with calmness, weakness and other so-called feminine attributes in many cultures today?

Actually, the history of the colour pink is fascinating; it has not always had the feminine association that it has today. Yet clothing manufacturers, journalists, celebrities and many others continue to quote the original Baker Miller pink research and some prisons in the world are painted pink today. Here's an insight into how the colour pink and femininity became so entwined in the 20th century.

Such is the power of culture and association!

I think it's helpful when creating our own designs that we ignore the myths and misinformation and focus instead on the idea that the power of colour is very much within the individual's experience. Once we have decided this, we can explore and discover YOUR special and individual relationship with colour. So let's get into the subject of colour families.

"Once pink had become associated in the United States with girls in the 1930s, the link became more and more powerful. Already conspicuous in the 1950s and 60s, when popular psychology encourages strong emphasis on distinct gender roles, the pinkification of girl culture really took off in the 1970s and 80s, when Mattel's Barbie acquired a new, predominantly pink wardrobe. By the end of the 20th century, the association of pink with girls had spread throughout the world."

Pink: The History of a Punk, Pretty, Powerful Colour.
Edited by Valerie Steele

Introducing the Six Colour families

Although there are so many factors to consider within colour psychology, we can analyse what each individual main colour and colour group is, which I've called 'colour families', means for you as an individual. And then we can find out which colour family or families you like the most. The human eye can detect and differentiate over one million colour hues. That's too much to label and identify. I have broken it down for you to just six colour families. I hope you agree that makes life much easier!

We know that great design involves choosing a selection of colours to use to create the right mood. Once upon a time there were specialist decorators that would mix a designer's perfect shade. Nowadays with modern technology, matching technology and the fact that most paint companies produce such sophisticated colour palette, this availability of colour choice is within everyone's reach.

Colour choice can be overwhelming because there are so many choices available. I use colour families to categorise and describe colours and to help my clients narrow it down. There are six colour families with simple labels. Each of these categories contain colours that go well together. Once you find the colour family or families you prefer, choosing paint colours becomes so much easier.

This is a really simplified method specifically designed to help people with low confidence in choosing colours. I've done this because I

Lakeside home in Finland

Colourful Caribbean house

find that most of the advice available in magazines and online is quite complex and sophisticated and, unhelpfully, assumes a lot of knowledge. A few of you may find this next section too basic or limited for you, and if you do, by all means skim over it. You can always come back later if you find you want to.

You can of course mix colours between the categories, but I warn you that it can be trickier to do and create a result that is still aesthetically pleasing.

You might find it helpful to think of colour schemes like seasons or climates around the globe. For example I invite you to imagine two very different scenes; a muddy autumn day in a wood in Scandinavia, and a bright sunny day near the sea in the Caribbean.

Both are beautiful but the colours are so different. This is because of the light values at different latitudes on the earth, as well as the time of year or season. You can see from the photos that the colours from each scene are very different, and in my view they would not mix well if combined across images. Humans are steeped in a history and evolution, and we visually know what naturally goes with what. When we create artificial environments in our homes, they work well when we don't deviate too far from nature's palette. And in fact there's an easy tip for you; use nature for inspiration and you won't go far wrong.

The Colours Families

1 Brights. These are primary and secondary colours that are bold, bright and fully saturated. Think of the colours of the rainbow: red, orange, yellow, green, blue, purple and violet. I also include fuchsia pink, lime green, and turquoise to this list. An example of a 'bright' is the bright yellow of the colour on a buttercup or daffodil. So bright and vibrant.

Sometimes, colours are so bright they are described as acid or fluorescent. Acid colours are great for a particular use like safety equipment. In my view they are not soft enough for the majority of home interiors, so I haven't included them in these descriptions. But, if you love acid brights, please do create an extra category and add them to your preferred list. They are perfect for creating a really energetic and exciting space.

Rainbow bedroom by Mel Hamblett

2 Darks. These are also sometimes known as shades and they are a combination of the bright colours above, with varying amounts of black added. An example of this is the colour of burgundy. So much darker and moody than bright red. You can have extremely dark colours or knock a colour back just a small amount depending on the effect you want to create. Perfect for creating a cosy or moody or relaxing space.

Dark lounge by Naomi Carroll

3 Pastels. Pastel colours are also sometimes called tints as they are a combination of the bright colours above with varying amounts of white added. An example is the colour of straw: pale and delicate. You can have extremely light colours or somewhere between mid-tone and light depending on the effect you want to create. Perfect for creating a calm and relaxing space.

Pastel lounge

4 Mids. These mid-hue colours are somewhere in between brights and pastels. Hence my term Mids. This hue is the hardest to describe with language and has the widest range of my colour families. An example is the colour of freshly churned butter. It's not bright yellow or pastel yellow. It's in the middle. These colours are clear and fresh. Perfect for creating a fresh, energetic space.

Mid-tone room

5. Muddy. These muddy or earthy hues have a brown undertone but are not anywhere near as dark as the dark colours. Tonally they are more like mids and have a wide range. They are warm and restful and very popular in interiors. A good example is dusky pink. It's not bright pink or pastel pink. It's a pink with a brown undertone. These colours are muddy and soft. Perfect for creating a relaxing environment.

Bedroom decorated in 'muddy' colours

White and wood room

Then we have:

6. Neutrals. These are called colours, but true neutrals are without colour. You would not see these in a rainbow or in nature. True neutrals are – White, Black and Grey.

In today's competitive home improvement market, paint companies are thinking of ways to help people pick colours. Most expand the 'neutral palettes' to include very pale pastels and very dark darks. Colours described as magnolia, mushroom, chocolate, mint, midnight and taupe would all fall into this category.

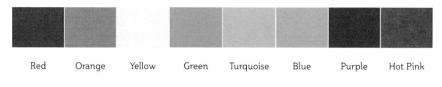

| Red | Orange | Yellow | Green | Turquoise | Blue | Purple | Hot Pink |

Brights

| Chocolate | Burgundy | Forest Green | Dark Teal | Midnight | Aubergine | Black Iris |

Darks

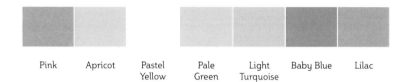

| Pink | Apricot | Pastel Yellow | Pale Green | Light Turquoise | Baby Blue | Lilac |

Pastels

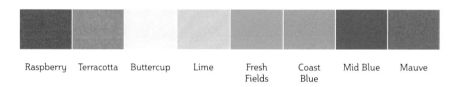

| Raspberry | Terracotta | Buttercup | Lime | Fresh Fields | Coast Blue | Mid Blue | Mauve |

Mid Tones

| Picante | Dusky | Sultry | Sand | Hay | In Deep | Khaki | Ocean |

Muddy

| Black | Brown | Brown Grey | Mid Grey | Taupe | Cream | White |

Neutrals

Warm colors

Cool colors

Colour wheel split in two showing warm and cool colours on either side

And finally, it's helpful to differentiate between warm and cool colours.

As you can see from the colour wheel, it has two sides: the warm side is made up of red, orange, and yellow and the cool side is made up of green, blue and violet. There is no evidence that I am aware of to suggest a link between personality types and warm or cool colours. It really depends on whether they are bright, dark, mid, or muddy version of that colour. Warm and cool colours exist in all of the first six categories, even in neutrals.

In general, schemes with warmer colours tend to be more energising and those with cooler colours are more calming. It is more complex though, as you can have cool reds and yellows, and warm blues and greens. My tip here is to be careful when mixing warm and cool colours, as the result is often jarring.

Some conclusions

Are you drawn to a particular palette? Look back at your moods from Chapter 8. Can you see a link between your colour family preference and the rest of your personality?

This is meant as a starting point. There are many more colour palettes to choose from, and there are many brilliant books available on the subject of colour, conjuring mood and colour psychology (see notes, resources and further reading section at the end of the book).

Once you feel that you have the basics of what you like, I encourage you to explore this subject further and expand your understanding of what might go with what.

Colour and language

One of the things I notice about colour conversations is how people use language to describe colour inconsistently. And it's not anybody's fault! In the English language we only have about fourteen words to describe colour where we have a good chance of describing something that is the same or similar and even then it's debatable. For example when you say lime green you are probably imagining a very different hue to when I think of lime green. It's green mixed with yellow, but how much green and how much yellow, and also there's a bit of white, so how much white?

I love the terms that paint companies come up with for colours don't you? And popular paint brand colours do enter common language. For example in the UK the Farrow and Ball paint colours of 'elephant's breath' (pale pinky grey) and 'down pipe' (mid to dark grey) are known by many of my friends, clients and fellow interior designers who enjoy using that brand.

Colour paint charts can be misleading. The best colour charts are painted with actual paint rather than a reproduction of

a colour. This helps prevent errors when putting design mood and sample boards together and, of course, a big test piece is helpful. I usually get a sample pot and paint a large piece of lining paper properly with two or three coats, to test what colour will look like in different parts of the room, in different lights and at different times of day. I use lining paper so I can move the sample around the room.

So far I've talked in general terms. But what about YOU? What is your relationship with different colours? Perhaps you know already? It's time to do a quiz and find out more.

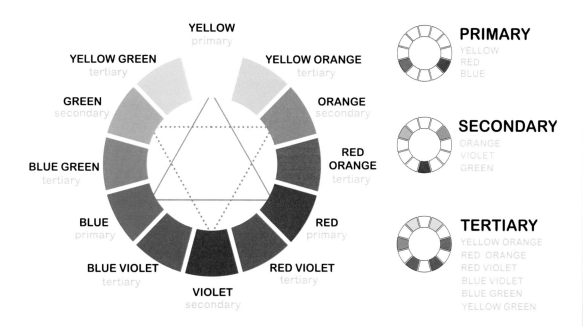

Colour wheel

Quiz time!

In this quiz, the questions are designed to raise your awareness from a contextual perspective, i.e. to help readers who have no idea what they like and don't like. If you know what colours you like, you will whizz through these questions. As with the other quizzes, try to answer quickly and instinctively.

Now I have described the colour families do you know which of these you like more than the others? Brights? Darks? Pastels? Mids? Muddy? Neutral?

Do you know which of these you like the least or would never use? Brights? Darks? Pastels? Mids? Muddy? Neutral?

What has been your favourite colour to use in interiors? Do you have a favourite combination of colours? How do you feel now after reading this chapter? Is it the same or have you added some new choices?

What colour do you never use? Do you know why?

Do you prefer warm (yellow based) or cool (blue based) colours?

Colour confidence

- Do you feel confident when choosing colours for a design?

- Do you decorate to please yourself or do you follow trends and copy magazines? Are you happy with your approach?

- In the past have you worried what others will think of your home and tone it down? Might you change this now? What will you do?

- Do you know what you like but find it difficult to put things together?

- Do you have a friend who is bolder in colour choice and you secretly wish you were too or are you happy as you are?

- Do you change your mind or would you say that once you make your mind up it stays fixed?

Final questions

- Do you want a style and colour scheme that runs through the whole house, or do you prefer to mix it up in different spaces?

- Are you aware of mood creation when you decorate? And what mood and colour formula you are using?

- What else have you realised through this process about your colour preferences?

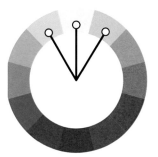

Harmonious
colour scheme

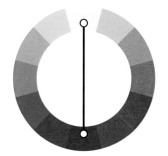

Complementary
colour scheme

Nature provides a
perfect colour palette

Hopefully, in answering these questions, you are uncovering your colour preferences and understanding your reactions to difference environments. I wonder if you are starting to see a pattern between your Big Five personality answers, your sensory dominance, your mood preferences and your values in relation to how you like colour.

And, if you are still struggling to find colour choices, here are some more ideas to help you find inspiration:

- Think of your favourite restaurant. What is the décor like? What colours are they using and in what proportion (of each colour)?

- Next time you go on a night out pay attention to the décor of the restaurants and bars you visit. What do you like and dislike?

- Is there a link between your clothing choices and your decorating style? What kind of colours do you like to wear?

- Where else do you get colour inspiration? You might think of fabrics, surface patterns, art, shop displays, online influences, getting out and about in nature, watching TV. What else might inspire you?

Remember, don't worry about whether you like or don't like a particular colour; instead, focus on your preferred colour families. Now you have some answers to that question, it's time to move on to colour combinations and explain the theory of how to put different colour schemes together.

Colour schemes explained

Introducing the colour wheel

As you can see from the labels, the colour wheel is made up of what's known as primary, secondary and tertiary colours. Primary colours are red, blue, and yellow, secondary colours are green, orange and purple, whilst tertiary colours are the next level of blend and where labels start to be trickier, i.e. turquoise or green-blue.

I have added nothing then black, white, more white and brown to create the colour families of brights, darks, mids, pastels, tints and muddy. Can you see how colour families work here?

Creating a scheme

Few people want to decorate a room in just one colour. If you were to paint everything in the same colour it would all blend together and create very little visual interest. So it's good to create a scheme for a room that has a combination of different colours; either within one colour family or mixing across families. Now you know your colour family preferences, it's time to take that information and add some complexity with potential colour combinations.

To start with I recommend that you totally or mainly stay in one family and place pastels with pastels, muddy with muddy, etc. It makes it much easier to get a colour scheme feeling right using this method. You can then choose any combination of colours within a family for your desired result; the two exceptions to this are neutrals and darks. Any of the other families will work with neutrals and darks, for example.

1 Dark blue with pastel yellow and pastel pink.

2 White and grey with mid coral pink.

Colour Combinations

So, how do you know how to put colours together if you struggle to do it instinctively? The answer is colour combinations. Colour combinations are divided into three main categories by artists and designers as follows, complementary, harmonious and monochromatic.

The colour families evoke different levels of brain stimulation, and in addition, colour combinations also create different levels of simulation. By looking at which mix of colour family and colour combination you want, you can get the stimulus and mood you desire exactly right, whether it be energising, exciting, sociable, fun, calming, relaxed, soothing, quiet or romantic.

Complementary

The first scheme type is called complementary and it's a classic! A complementary scheme chooses colours that are opposite each other across the colour wheel. For example, red – green, or orange – blue and yellow - purple.

An interesting phenomenon happens when these complementary colours are placed next to each other. Each colour appears more vibrant; the colours sing! This produces a bold and stimulating effect in an interior. The brighter the colours, the bolder the impact! This kind of scheme is a good choice for rooms where lots of energy is required like cooking and socialising. It suits

Showroom complimentary colours display

spaces designed for extroverted activity or an extrovert personality. It is also appropriate for learning and working environments for some personalities.

Mood: Stimulating and energising especially with brights or mids.

This type of room is suitable for extraverts or for introverts who want a room decorated to reflect the sociable activities that will occur in that space.

Adjacent or harmonious scheme

An adjacent scheme is a scheme where the colours used are adjacent, i.e. next to each other on the colour wheel. For example, yellow and yellow-green (lime green).

Choosing colours that are very close to each other in hue creates a harmonious look and feel. This look can be achieved using warm or cool colours as well as

brights or muddy colours. The drama and energy is managed by the brightness and saturation of colour choice, rather than the contrast between the colours.

This type of room scheme energy is usually calming but the level will depend on the vibrancy of the colours chosen. For example, warm harmonious bright hues of red orange and yellow is a more energetic choice than a scheme of cool pastels of blue and green. This scheme has the versatility to suit all personality types.

Clashing colours?

Some interior and fashion designers describe colours as clashing. This usually means that they are bright and vibrant and close to each other on the colour wheel. A good example would be cherry red and cerise pink. In colour theory terms they are close together on the colour wheel, which makes

Harmonious room scheme in dimmed light, white, blues and purples

them 'harmonious'. However the high saturation and brightness is so impactful people like to use the word clashing. It's confusing, isn't it?!

Monochromatic

A monochromatic scheme is a scheme using one colour but different tints or shades of that colour. For example, to create a colour plus lighter tones add various amounts of white to the main colour to create hues that are mids to pastels. And for darker shades add various amounts of black to create mids to darks. Paint companies often produce charts of tints and shades to make this really easy for customers to choose. It's the easiest scheme to think through and

is usually very calming and harmonious to the spirit. It's an understated and subtle look. Be careful, though, although this is harmonious, it also has the potential lack of any interest. It's harder to highlight focal points in a room if there is too little contrast. One way to manage this is to have a mainly harmonious scheme with a few pops of a complimentary opposite colour, e.g. three blues at different intensities and one complementary orange that matches one of the blues tonally.

Mood: Depends on proportions of colour used and how bright the base colour is. Usually calming.

If you are introverted and a high kinaesthetic you might enjoy this room

Clashing colours. Could you imagine the vibrancy of a room decorated in these stunning red and fuchsia dahlias? It would be incredibly stimulating.

A cool Scandinavian series of blues in this Monochromatic room

that has lots of layered textures and variable lighting to add interest.

High Contrast

For those scoring high on extraversion or openness to experience there is an alternative to using colour for creating stimulus and that is high contrast. High contrast creates drama without colour or just a little colour. A classic example is black and white. These colours become more dramatic when put together. Imagine a checkerboard floor and then imagine an all-black floor. There is much more interest and drama in the checkerboard. Art deco is a good example of a style that makes use of the high-contrast approach to design. And don't worry if you don't like black and

white; high contrast isn't limited to those two. Other examples are navy and cream, dark green and pale yellow; and there are many examples from which you can choose. As long as you have a very dark shade combined with a very light tint and a limited palette you will have created high contrast.

A note on numbers of colours and proportions

Now you know about different combinations of colours, it's important to understand what proportions to use. Scale and proportion is an important part of design and this applies to using colour in a room too. You may wonder, how many colours do I need? The answer is that most schemes have 3 - 5

Choose one colour as the dominant colour

60%

Walls, floors, dominant fabrics, and furniture

Choose one colour as an intermediate colour

30%

Ceilings, cabinets, floors and smaller furniture

Incorporate one or two accent colours

10%

Trim and moulding, pillows, rugs and accessories

main colours. More than one and less than five is a good rule of thumb.

As important as how many colours you put in your scheme is the proportion in which you use them. If you use two colours in a 50/50 split, this can create a visual competition which tires the eyes. This is even more pronounced if the colours are complimentary opposites. A good guide is to have a dominant colour and a secondary colour. And then you may also want to add in a small dramatic third. So, either 70/20/10 or 60/30/10 are good guides for proportion. If you feel like breaking this rule, start small and build it up.

How colours affect each other

Mood boards and sample boards are very helpful when working out how colours combine as some colours look very different when placed next to another colour (more on this in Chapter 16).

One of the reasons that mood boards are so essential is because they highlight how colours look when they are placed next to each other. For example orange can look more yellow when placed by red, but more orange when placed by yellow. With colour it's always good to check the context.

I have tried my best to slim down the advice and choices to make your life easier. It isn't easy! Hopefully by now, you have a good idea of which colour family and colour schemes best suit your personality. Of all the options the highest drama will be achieved with bright colours and complementary schemes or darks, lights or neutrals and a high contrast scheme. The calmest room of all will be low contrast, monochrome or harmonious, using darks, neutrals or pastel colours. Somewhere in the middle are an infinite number of combinations!

Fresh and pretty, spring-inspired mood board by Zoe Hewett

Calm drama and high contrast in this black and white double-height space

Design Tips

Here are some design tips for using your different colour preferences in interiors.

Design tips for those who prefer decorating with neutrals and pastels

The fact that you prefer neutral colour schemes probably means that you like to feel calm, relaxed, rested and peaceful a lot of the time, and especially at home. Neutral schemes are a strong favourite with a lot of people. Especially if they desire a sanctuary space and contrast to a stressful job/busy life. It is also traditionally the Landlord and Estate Agents choice as they think it will appeal to the majority of people and it is easy to refresh (for property owners). But this can be frustrating for renters who cannot redecorate and is seen as too boring and lacking in personality by colour fans. If you choose neutrals because you love them, I wholeheartedly support you. However, if you choose neutrals because you think they are a safe choice, stop! Please review the colour families and try to be a little more adventurous. If you lack confidence why not start small and build up your new look gradually.

- Suits introverts personality types; High conscientious scorers. People with a high need for safety and security.

- Suits activities like sleeping, therapy, treatments, relaxing, reading, tv, meditation, concentration.

- Suits many spaces such as lounges, bedrooms, offices, therapy spaces.

A neutral interior

Design tips for those who like the 'Brights' colour family

You love using bright colours, these are hues with full saturation and vibrancy. When bright colours are used in a room scheme design, the energy levels are ramped up. Bright colours include primary, secondary and tertiary colours that are fully saturated and those that are just knocked back a little bit by adding a small amount of black, white or grey.

The fact that you have chosen these colours as your preferred palette suggests you like to be in spaces where the mood is energised, excited, playful and sociable. This look is very popular for both residential and public spaces. Make sure the tonal value matches in order to keep the vibrancy high.

- Suits high extrovert personality types, high openness to experience. Visual.

- Suits activities like eating, playing, socialising, talking, working, selling, creating.

- Suit spaces such as kitchens, bathrooms, garden rooms, offices, art studios, workshops, kids bedroom or playroom, dining areas.

Layer-up the look for added impact. For example, very colourful sofas and chairs, add vibrant colourful artwork

Bright and contrasting colours

and add patterns and unusual lighting and colourful rugs. Consider everything as an option to add colour.

Design tips for those who prefer the 'Darks' colour family

You have said that you prefer schemes made up of darker colours and shades. This design style requires quite a lot of confidence to pull off but can be very effective. The key is to go all dark. If you leave some pale or white space you will end up with contrast which is not what you want. It's important to think through all the spaces including the ceiling and the floor. It's not just about painting the walls. The moods created are very similar to neutrals but with a bit more drama. The dominant moods by immersing a space in all dark colours include; feeling relaxed, sultry, romantic, safe, restful and calm.

- Suits introvert personality types. Low Openness to Experience. High conscientiousness. The urge to be safe. This darker look may appeal to highly sensitive person as it creates feelings of cosiness and safety.

- Suits activities like sleeping, therapy, treatments, relaxing, reading, TV, meditation, concentration.

- Suits many spaces such as lounges, bedrooms, offices, therapy spaces.

Muddy and mid tone colour family interiors

These last two colour-family interiors are much easier to get right when you keep your eye on getting the proportions and numbers of colours right for the space. These interiors suit many moods, activities and personality types.

Combinations

By now, if not before, you will hopefully be aware just how many different combinations you could pull together. The different colour scheme combinations can be used to create or reduce drama. The value of paint colour and numbers of different colours you use will do the same. And, of course,

this is just about colour. There are other ways that you can create the feel or moods you want, which we will cover in the next chapter.

I hope I've given you some tried and tested methods for creating the look and feel that you want and the confidence to use them to create a space you love.

More design tips regarding colour use for all personalities

In order to complete this chapter on colour I have included some design tips using colour that apply no matter what your personality. There is a lot to discover if this subject interests you.

The impact of colour and colour psychology in interior design impacts us in the following four ways. Let's go through each in turn:

1 Individual personality type and level of emotional stimulation: The level of emotional stimulation or mood that a colour evokes in you is unique to you because of your personality. Your emotional response is likely to be instant and instinctive; and it will influence whether you want to stay or leave a space and how long you want to be in it.

2 Individual personality type and physical and/or mental stimulation: The level of physical reaction that

An example of how to create a focal point. See how the yellow chair stands out against the white, grey and black

a colour evokes in you is also unique to you even though it is also partly hard-wired and shared by everyone. Colour has been shown to change behavioural responses; for example people can feel a change of appetite, a change in state of relaxation, or a change in temperature perception in a space depending on what colour it is decorated in.

3   All personalities - creates visual distortions: Colour affects our perception of space and sometimes this leads to visual distortions. The level of impact of visual distortion will be a combination of your personal reaction and a common reaction across everyone. Designs and colour use can make a room seem smaller, bigger, wider and longer. We can use colour to

deliberately change our visual perception to suit a space design. It can be fun to choose to use colour in design in this way.

4   All personalities - makes a statement and creates focus: When combined with lighting, the use of colour can create or magnify objects creating focal points in a space. The level of impact of lighting and colour combined is a combination of your personal reaction and a common reaction across everyone. Lighting design uses colour in light to display and show off prize objects, personality, taste, politics, nationality, even spiritual or cultural beliefs.

Colour and perception

Red, orange and yellow are not only warm, but they are also known as advancing colours, which means that they appear closer to the viewer because of their hue. Wherever they are used they will appear closer to the eye and attract more attention. Yellow is the most attention grabbing of all, followed by orange and then red. In contrast, a receding colour is one which does the opposite; it gives the perception of receding. It appears further away and is less prominent to view. Examples of receding colours are purple and blue. If you use yellow and blue together, blue will appear further away. Green is

The dark ceiling help make this
space feel more intimate

in the middle range, neither advancing, nor receding. Green is often seen as a balancing colour as it visually 'holds' the middle ground.

The impact of this phenomenon of advancing or receding is more pronounced in brights and mids compared to dark, muddy and pastel colours.

Visual effects

You can use your new knowledge of advancing and receding colours to good effect in design to suit your purposes, especially if you have a challenging space to decorate.

Room shapes and size

The choice of colour will affect the way a space is perceived as well as the mood it creates. We see the world as a picture through our eyes, and our brain interprets that picture perceiving depth, size and volume. If you have an odd-shaped room or want to solve a problem of lack of light, then colour is your powerful ally. For example if you have a room which is long and thin, and you want an end wall to appear nearer to you, then painting it yellow will do

that for you. However, if you want to accentuate the length of the room and create the sensation that the end wall is further away, painting it blue will help.

If you want to make a small room look larger, a generally accepted rule is that paler colours work better than darker ones. Another way to fool the eye is to remove the eyes ability to see the edges by painting all surfaces the same colour; you literally can't see the edges. Low contrast in a room can increase its feeling of space, but it doesn't matter if the colour is white, light or dark. The effect will work with all colours and it can work really well with dark colours. Some people worry that making a room dark will make it seem smaller. And this

Paint can change the size of a room

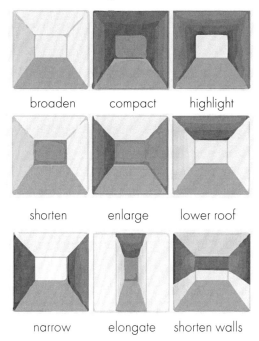

broaden   compact   highlight

shorten   enlarge   lower roof

narrow   elongate   shorten walls

Dark and calm lounge scheme

puts them off. However, if you paint all the walls the same colour, sometimes this makes a room feel endless. This is especially true if you paint the ceiling dark as well. Pools of light then can be created with gentle artificial lamps of warm white light.

To make a space feel more intimate you can create a visual illusion of bringing the ceiling down to you by painting the ceiling a darker colour. This is especially helpful in rooms with high ceilings. The illusion is even more effective when you paint down the sides of the wall to a picture rail or a line that mimics the rail.

Features and colour blocking

A common habit for most people is to paint the walls one colour, the ceiling white/off white, and the paint work white/off white. Sometimes people paint a feature wall in a different colour, or perhaps alcoves in a different colour. There's nothing wrong with this approach, but I wonder why we've settled into this pattern. When you stop and think about it you may not want to highlight the edges of the room.

There is a different approach called colour blocking which was popular in the 1960s and its popularity has resurfaced in recent years, where you can use paint in a different way to make

145

A colour blocking circle

a space feel different using only colour and shapes. Using blocks of colours is a great way to achieve a number of aims, including: helping to zone spaces or emphasise a particular area or activity in a room; injecting a vibrant and highly saturated colour into a room with just a small pop of it to draw attention to particular features, e.g. fireplace or window recess; or draw attention away from less desirable objects in a room, such as a television. The idea is to use shapes and colour blocks independently of the room corners and edges. You use paint to draw the eye to where you want it and where you want people to pay attention.

Natural light and room direction

In the northern hemisphere the light in a north-facing room is cool and has greener tones, whereas south-facing rooms are warm with violet tones. If you decorate a cooler room in cool or neutral or pastel paint colours, the natural light will emphasise any cool pigments in that paint. If you don't want this effect then using colours from the warm end of the colour spectrum will help to warm up the space. Any bright or mid reds and oranges will work. As long as there is red in the base it will be warm. Apply the opposite principle for the southern hemisphere.

If you have a lack of natural light in a space, the temptation may be to paint the room in a white or very light colour. Unfortunately, the lack of light might still make the room look dingy and grey.

Instead, try a warm-based colour in a mid or brighter hue and use test pots before you commit. In addition, warm (yellow toned white rather than blue) artificial lighting will bring light to this space day and night.

Context

How a colour appears will depend on the context including, natural light levels, your perception, the time of day, and what other colours surround it. For example, a window overlooking a green lawn and trees will reflect green light into the room.

The quality of materials matters

How a colour appears will also depend on the quality of the paint, binders, dyes, mordants and materials used in the paint. More expensive paints cost more because they have a higher % content of natural pigments which will reflect the light, which changes at different times of day. The result is that they feel sumptuous and rich and they're worth every penny in my view. Matching colours does work but is not as vibrant as the original in many cases. However, how much you want to spend on paint will depend on your budget as well as your taste. There are many good quality paints available in the middle price range, and plenty of colours to choose from. My advice is to avoid the cheap end though, because the colours are nowhere near as good and the coverage is poor. You may repent your decision to go cheap as you are painting the fourth coat! I am talking from painful experience here!

Pulling it together (so far...)

In summary, there are quite a lot of things to pull together when deciding on a colour scheme. Firstly, think about the function of the room. What activities will you be mainly doing there? Then think about the people who will be using that room and their personality type. Finally, think about what mood you want to conjure with your scheme. You now have the main ingredients you need to design and create your ideal home:

- Your personality scores.

- Your dominant sense(s).

- The functional need.

- Your preferred mood(s).

- Your preferred colour family and colour scheme(s).

- Any quirks of the space(s) you need to consider (e.g. lack of light, odd shape).

The lounge scheme of an extrovert with a high level of agreeability and a love of hosting may have a complementary colour lounge scheme with fairly vibrant colours because it is the space where they will entertain guests.

However, the same person may prefer a pastel monochrome bedroom look, in tints of blue and white, because this is a space where they want to relax and go to sleep.

I hope this section has given you a lot of clarity about what kind of colour schemes you like and dislike. Remember, that you may want very different looks in different rooms of your house.

Please do fill out this colour section on your personality summary sheet from Chapter 2 with your thoughts and ideas. And finally some additional areas of consideration that might appeal to some.

When researching this chapter I reviewed a lot of information in the colour psychology and colour therapy fields. Although they aren't particularly relevant for guiding you towards your design personality here is some additional information that you may find of interest. I have also included some recommended reading at the end of the book for those of you that want to find out more.

Colour symbolism

Sometimes when people start to talk to me about colour psychology, I realise what they are really talking about is colour symbolism. These two subjects are not the same. As I explained earlier, the culture and country we grow up in influences our response to colour. Each society or culture has developed associations between colours and responding emotions. And, sometimes these go deep, but not as deep as the

instincts in relation to colour which all humankind share.

Ideas like pink is relaxing and romantic, or yellow is cheerful, have mixed response results in scientific research. The responses to these two colours differ between people, content and cultures, so it is important to remain cautious about correlations you hear about between colours and corresponding colour responses. I think it's more important to focus on in YOUR response to a colour. Do you find pink relaxing and romantic? And do you want that feeling? Do you find bright yellow cheerful and vibrant? And do you want to feel energised? It's your home, and your choice.

Colour therapy and spirituality

The Indian chakra system and many other spiritual systems have a colour-based descriptor and Chromotherapists use colour in therapy and healing. For example it is believed that green light can help relieve stress and relax a person. I think that spiritual theories that have existed for hundreds and sometimes thousands of years are a fascinating area. It's very much a personal choice and mostly person centred; although it can extend to physical environment. For those of you that are interested in finding out more on the subject I have added resources and book references at the end of this book.

Exercise

Now you have completed this section on colour it's time to fill in the summary sheet in Chapter 2. You may also want to make some notes around the following questions.

- What is your preferred colour family?

- Which of the colour schemes appealed the most?

- Do you prefer a home to be calm, lively or a mixture of both?

- How do your colour preferences link in with your other personality aspects and choices so far?

- What thoughts or ideas did the chapter raise? Write it down on your summary

Chapter summary

Colour is a powerful and relatively inexpensive way to create dramatic transformations in interior design. In this chapter we have discussed the science behind how we perceive colour, explored the colour spectrum and the colour wheel. We've understood how colour impacts our emotional, mental health and physical being and our perception of our environment. I've introduced you to the ideas of colour families and colour combinations to help you build your own colour schemes, and explained how colour schemes contribute to creating a desired mood. Towards the end of the chapter we have discussed how colour can be used to create visual illusions and the difference between colour psychology and colour symbolism.

Chapter 11

Forms and styles

After colour, the style of design is the second most popular thing that people like to talk about in terms of interiors. Often people like a fusion between two or more styles. And some people are truly eclectic, mixing items from many different eras and design aesthetics. When people lack confidence with colour they often also lack confidence on selecting items that ascetically go together style wise. In this chapter I will explore and breakdown what makes a style, and help you understand what styles you like and dislike to further increase your confidence in putting together your own design schemes.

What are forms and styles?

Sometimes people will describe an interior style using mood words like soft, romantic, edgy or soothing. Other times the descriptions are more specific, identifiable and labelled; mid-century modern, industrial, cottage core.

All architectural and interior design styles can be descriptively deconstructed into forms and shapes like curves, spheres, straight lines and cubes. When you understand styles and forms, you can start to unpick what makes up 'a look'; and make decisions on furniture, wallpaper and flooring more easily because you will know what goes with what and how these styles, when combined with other factors like lighting, colour and layout, can help to create a mood or feeling in a space.

The architecture at Marrakesh Airport

Unique and Historic. Glorious shape and form in action: the Art Deco hotels at South Beach, Miami

Shapes and forms

Let's start with shapes. Shapes (sometimes called forms) in this context are either internal structures and objects, or external outlines in rooms and buildings, usually in a 3D shape like a sphere or cube.

An architect or designer looks at a project from the perspective of solving issues and developing solutions for the user using forms and shapes. Form can be simplified as follows:

- Shape – form outline.

- Size – form dimensions, proportions and scale.

- Colour – the colour of the form will affect its visual weight (darker = heavier).

- Texture – the texture of a form will affect how light is reflected or absorbed.

- Position and orientation – where the form is in relation to the ground, compass points and viewer.

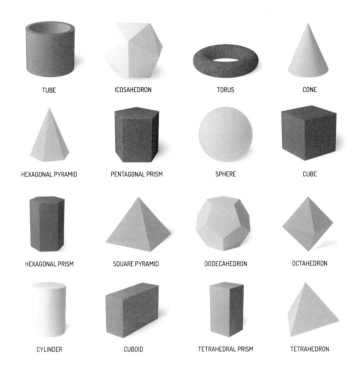

TUBE   ICOSAHEDRON   TORUS   CONE

HEXAGONAL PYRAMID   PENTAGONAL PRISM   SPHERE   CUBE

HEXAGONAL PRISM   SQUARE PYRAMID   DODECAHEDRON   OCTAHEDRON

CYLINDER   CUBOID   TETRAHEDRAL PRISM   TETRAHEDRON

Architecture school -
building blocks

Styles and trends come and go

In the built environment the forms and styles associated with historical styles such as Roman, Egyptian and Greek classical architecture have been repeated many times over the centuries. The Victorians were especially good at borrowing styles from the past. In each era humankind looks forward and backwards, and fashions come and go. In interiors, following trends and fashion is synonymous with the fashion industry. You will have your own individual preferences which go beyond fashion. Trends and fashions can be confusing anyway. You don't need to know what's 'on trend' because, in this chapter, I will demystify styles and help you discover what you like and don't like. The answers will be, in all likelihood, in line with your other personality-led choices.

The house that you live in will probably reflect the architectural style that was dominant in the time that your house was constructed. And, of course, each country has different construction methods and styles too. Ideally we are able to live in a home that suits us and our personality. In a way the personality of your home's style and your own personality forms a relationship – a fusion. This is a relationship where you get to dominate, but, hopefully, you will do it sympathetically. Personally, nothing saddens me more than someone who buys an old property and then takes out all the original features because they like a modern style. But I'm getting ahead of myself. Let's talk about style.

What styles are popular today?

At the time of writing this book in 2022, there are many named interior design styles that are popular in interiors. These styles can suit many different types of property. Some examples include industrial, art deco, minimalist, boho, rustic and mid-century modern.

Here are two styles on trend and yet very different in look and feel. Each of these elements can be broken down into the constituent parts that make up its style. The skill of a designer (and now hopefully you too) is to pull together a look that achieves the aims of the homeowner, and is both aesthetically pleasing and consistent. Get it right and items look like they're meant to go together and the whole look is pleasing. Get it wrong and a design can look messy or disconnected. Paying attention to forms and styles is an important part of the design process.

Styles and the creation of a mood

Style details are an important influence in evoking mood within a space. For example, geometric shapes and straight lines can give an efficient, hard and no-nonsense feel to a space. These shapes are suitable for more formal environments and work environments when it's helpful to have barriers and structure, such as a courtroom or a police interview room.

Conversely curves, circles, fans, details like frills, carvings and spheres are usually linked with softer environments, where the mood is more informal, friendly and intimate. If you look at a style and then look at the shapes and understand your own

Modern maximalist tablescape in dark colours

Space and proportion: Creating a lighting fitting to suit this long spiral staircase and get the scale and proportion right is tricky. The designer has opted for smaller light shades and lots of them. The effect is like beads of water dripping down a wire. By picking a delicate smaller light feature, the size and scale and swirls of the staircase are emphasised.

Neutral rustic minimalist dining

emotional responses, you start to understand how the style creates the mood.

Scale and proportion

When choosing furniture and fittings, it's important to understand and think about the impact of the scale of shapes and forms within the space. Architects and designers use rules of scale and proportion to appropriately design details such as skirting, doorways, mouldings, etc. You can do the same in the interiors. Sometimes, however, it's fun to play with proportions. Oversized items can add desired drama because they are disproportionate to the space. If you feel unsure about this, it's ok to stick to a scale that is proportional.

Style inspiration: using Pinterest and other social media platforms.

Do you know what styles of interiors you like and don't like? Or are you wondering how to identify them? One way is to look through magazines and collect images of rooms that you like, or go online and create a Pinterest board or boards of favourite images.

Pinterest and Instagram are incredibly useful sources of inspiration and imagery. Searching through the sites can be fruitful, but it can also be frustrating because you might end up with too many pictures and no idea what to do with them all. Feeling overwhelmed by options is inevitable after too much searching. My advice here is to enjoy collecting lots of ideas, then leave it alone for a few days. Then, when you return to your ideas fresh, you will hopefully feel you will have a new perspective and you can edit and streamline your content ruthlessly, so you will then have a more manageable selection.

You can do this digitally if you prefer. But the traditional way is fun too: cutting and pasting. Either way you can select items from various places, i.e. you may like the sofa from one space, the lamp from another and so on.

I've put together a couple of quizzes to help you to understand what you like in terms of interior styles. The first is about shapes and forms in the abstract, the second is actual styles, and I have added some photographs to help you. You should be able to do these really easily now you have so much self-awareness!

I'm building a picture of your taste with you in a deliberate order. There is so much choice in the world of interiors; going straight to styles and photographs of interiors can be overwhelming and tricky. By waiting until now to do the styles quizzes, you should be able to select things you like and dislike much more quickly.

Let's have a go.

This Pieminister restaurant is a great example of the industrial pared back aesthetic with bare lights, bare brick walls, wire enclosed spaces, wood and metal seats, and dark painted ceiling and fittings. This space feels intimate because of the dark colour scheme and dimmed lighting.

Quiz time!

Back to basic forms and styles

This quiz is all about back to basics. As with the other quiz please answer as quickly as possible without thinking too much.

What do you prefer?	Preferably select one, but if you like both choose both
Clean lines or curves?	
Patterned or plain fabric/wallpaper?	
Matt or slight sheen or glossy surfaces?	
Stripes or floral fabric/wallpaper?	
Contemporary or nostalgic/ old-fashioned styles?	
Symmetrical or organic layouts?	
Smooth or textured surfaces?	
Natural or more modern materials?	
Luxurious or rustic?	
Country or city?	
Casual or smart?	

Look at your answers. Do they go together? For example, floral, curves and nostalgic would go together well. Another collection might be plain, natural, down-to-earth.

Also, it's worth noticing where they don't go together. You might like to have the same look in every room or conversely, you might have a preference for different looks for different environments, circumstances or moods. This will probably be linked to how high your openness to experience score was. The higher the score, the more you will seek variety in your environment. As already discussed, some people like change and variety more than others. Make a note of your styles and preferences for the spaces in your home (and work if appropriate) on your summary sheet.

Styles

Now you've done the 'back to basics' exercise, we are ready to look at named styles. Look at each label and album of pictures I think reflect that style.

For each set of images ask yourself what you like and dislike about that particular style. This time I do want you to think a bit more. React to it instinctively at first, and then think about why you have had that reaction.

For example, I love coastal décor because it reminds me of my childhood living by the sea. The colours are gentle but not washed out. They are of the sea, sky and sand. I like lots of wood and other natural materials as well as pictures of nature and seascapes.

The slightly battered furniture with layers of paint and history gives me a sense of calm and relaxation. There's a lot of comfort, textures, soft wools and cottons. Natural light everywhere. Nothing to do there but curl up in a chair with a book and breathe deeply.

Here are some examples of popular styles today

There are many styles of décor. These are just a few I picked out. Have I missed one that you really love? if so, please add it to your summary sheet and describe what it is that you like about it in style form, linking back to you personality preferences.

Classical (Greeks and Roman influence).
This lounge has many features of a classically designed and traditional space, including wall panelling, fireplaces, beams, grand book cases, chandelier and practical quality furniture lighting and materials.

There is a feast of natural materials in this country cottage; wooden beams, brick and stone walls, window frame and floor; earthware and baskets.

Art Deco lounge space in dark green with pale pink. This dramatic high contrast scheme has geometric lines and hints of gold for a touch of luxury.

Floral: this is a bold pink floral scheme. Heaven for some! The long sumptuous curtains match the wallpaper and the solid bright pink chair fabric and lampshade are confident. The plainer flooring and ceiling offer some calm into this stimulating design.

This coastal-inspired bedroom has a limited palette of bright white and icy blue. The layers of bedding, throws and rustic textures in the baskets add a sense of comfort to this fresh look. The oversized palm injects a moment of drama and the ornaments emphasise the coastal theme.

This luxurious hotel bathroom is spacious and sumptuously decorated in marble, ceramics and glass. The gold bowls are highlighted against the black marble and the glass chandeliers are subtle yet still sparkly in the dimmed light. The roll top bath takes centre stage in the alcove inviting residents to enjoy some pamper time.

This neutral rustic space has a simple design and timeless feel, with white walls, a wood floor and vintage or reclaimed furniture and fittings in iron and wood. The overall effect is pared back yet charming.

This gorgeous Mid Century Modern Scandart rocking chair is a result of a Facebook market place find by designer, Hannah Redden, upholstery by Sarah of Wisteria Workshop, and velvets from Linwood Fabrics.

A perfect home for a industrial aesthetic-loving busy city dweller

The same principle applies to all details in furniture and fittings: light switches, architrave, skirting boards, window treatments, door handles, etc. As you then go on to choose fabrics, lighting and ornaments, you can choose to follow ideas using the same shapes and forms there as well.

Building up your confidence

You can mix styles, but, if you are unsure how to, I suggest you stick to one style to start with, or maybe put your ideas and selections down on a sample board to help you see what your ideas will look like in real life. Doing this before you spend any money will reduce frustrations as mixing styles can be difficult to pull off.

It will help you evaluate scale and proportion to suit your space too. Another way to build your confidence with interiors, is to layer up the look bit by bit. Start with the essentials like layouts, lighting plans, flooring and fabrics for furniture and window treatments in one main style and colour way and then add a variety of styles in accessories and wall art gradually. Changing a lamp or a rug or cushion is much cheaper than replacing flooring or a sofa or work surface!

Here are a couple of design tips for the popular styles of 'industrial' and 'country rustic'.

Design tips for industrial style

The industrial style in interiors has been popular for a while now. The elements that make up this style are inspired by factories and industrial spaces. Here are some tips to help you to create this style at home:

- Create a back to basic structured space with everything on show. For example, you can see pipe work and unfinished surfaces like concrete and bricks.

- Use a neutral or dark colour palette. This style is really devoid of colour. If you want drama, add high contrasts with black and white, or grey and white. If you want less drama keep colours more harmonious and similar in tone.

- Think clean lines, straight lines, angular shapes.

- Use natural and raw materials: concrete, wood, metals, leather, bricks, stone. These materials add lots of texture, and that makes up for the lack of colour because textures help throw the light around and this adds interest to the interior.

- This look can go with both a minimalist and a maximalist approach depending on your preference.

The story that supports this look is a busy city dweller with a sophisticated cultural life filled with business or art or music. Home is a quiet respite from their busy life.

In the picture opposite the hard edges and materials have been softened with lots of plants, books and soft touches such as cushions and throws.

In personality terms this home is ideal for someone who is an ambivert or an introvert, with a high level of conscientiousness, medium to low agreeability, and who has a visually dominated sensory life.

Design tips for country rustic style

This is a popular and timeless style that is inspired by a simpler life, close to nature and full of natural materials that are rough, aged and worn. Here are some tips to help you to create this style at home.

The elements that make up this style include:

- A cosy and comfortable space where everything has texture, be it rough or soft.

- A number of colour palettes suit this style. It could be pastels or mid hue, some bold colours and even all white. Nothing too dark though. Often schemes are inspired by natures palette.

- Everything you choose will have soft lines, curves, irregular shapes.

Make sure you add in lots of soft furnishings, from heavy sumptuous curtains, sink into sofas and lots and lots of cushions.

- Choose artwork that is inspired by nature, with landscapes and images of flowers birds and animals.

- Materials are all natural. The truly rustic look is made up of: cotton, wool, wood, ceramics, stone, glass. Minimal use of metal and synthetics like plastic.

- This look can go with both a minimalist and a maximalist approach depending on your preference.

The story that supports this look is a countryside and nature lover. In the spring and summer windows are flung open, jars are full of flowers, there is a sense of making the most of home produce in abundance with lots of cooking, homemade cordials and jelly, jams and pickles. In winter, the log fire is burning and homeowners and animals all snuggle in from the storm outside, with the dogs snoozing after a long walk and a roast lunch.

In personality terms this style ideal is for someone scoring medium to high on openness to experience, medium to low on conscientiousness and highly kinaesthetic.

An abundance of vegetables are on the chopping board in Kath's pretty cottage kitchen.

Exercise

Forms, styles and personality types

So now you have some answers around what kind of styles you like and why, you can add this information to your personality summary. Your summary is getting really full now isn't it? My advice is to pick a maximum of four of all these styles to add to your summary. More than that will get too busy. You can combine styles depending on how confident you're feeling.

Although you have a lot of information about what you like, you also have the hidden knowledge about what you don't like, or want, which will be most helpful in narrowing down design choices.

What additional thoughts or ideas did the chapter or quiz raise? Write it down on your summary too.

Chapter summary

In this chapter we have discussed styles, what makes up different styles, and how styles and form impact mood and reflect personality preferences in a scheme. Hopefully now you have selected your preferred styles and forms and you've added this to your summary. You may have found links and had some 'aha' moments about how your personality scores and dominant sense and desired mood all come together and are expressed in your style preferences. We have almost completed a full design process. Almost! Just a couple more things to consider.

Chapter 12

Values and beliefs

When we feel strongly about an aspect of our personality it also forms part of our self-image or identity. We are strongly attached to that part of ourselves. The objects we surround ourselves with serve to reinforce our sense of self and this is an important part of creating the 'at home' feeling. When people say they feel 'at home' it's a complex mixture of feelings including, happiness, safety, validation, comfort and relaxation.

Personality is just one of many different elements that make up a human being's sense of identity. A lot of personality traits are revealed through behaviour and attitude, so we can evaluate someone else's personality fairly easily by interacting with them. But not everything is on show. Some elements are more hidden. These elements are our values, beliefs and motivation.

What we believe and what we feel are important in life are based on values that are sometimes unknown to us. These beliefs are often picked up in early childhood from close and extended family and then from friends, educators and other influences as we grow up. Some values and beliefs impact what kind of environments we create and enjoy.

Here is an example of a set of beliefs you might hear as a child. How do you think these beliefs might impact your home style, décor and taste?

- Rich people are greedy
- Materialism is corrupt
- Family is everything
- You can't buy love

This large spacious and well appointed 'outdoor' kitchen has all you need for a luxury, high status gathering. Perfect for someone who has a mix of both hosting and status values. Fancy a dip in the pool?

An attractive vignette from Nook Interiors

In my work, wealth and luxury are particularly contentious subjects. But they need not be. Here are two examples of childhood experiences for you to consider. Can you predict the outcome on the tastes of these two women now they are adults?

Belief 1: Rich people are awkward

A little girl visits her Grandparents once a month for afternoon tea. The home is formal, luxurious and expensively decorated. Everything is high-end quality: Axminister patterned carpets, original art, crystal and china in glass cabinets and the smells of daily cleaning activity. Even the little doll in the bathroom hiding the toilet roll has a serious rather than playful job to do. See the little girl sitting politely on the edge of an expensive sofa awkwardly holding a cup and saucer and answering questions about school. The china is beautiful and delicate. The biscuits are posh and delicious. The feelings evoked by the atmosphere and the surroundings for the little girl are awkwardness, fear of saying something wrong, or spilling the tea. Anxiety floods her little system as strongly as if she were sitting an exam at school.

Luxurious hotel lobby

Belief 2: Rich people can afford to buy the best materials and get exactly what they want

A little girl looks forward to visiting her Grandparents with excitement. They were often renovating and she was sometimes invited to give her opinion. She particularly remembers being invited to join in with conversations when they were choosing a new kitchen. They could afford a bespoke design and expensive marble work surface. The cupboard doors they chose were beautiful solid oak and crafted by an experienced cabinet maker. The lighting, flooring, crockery and glassware were glossy and beautifully made. In all these situations she was listened to and respected for her views. She loved seeing the choices come to life in the renovations.

How might these two individuals approach wealthy and luxurious environments as adults? Which of these experiences is truer of you? Imagine you were teleported from where you are now reading this book and placed in an expensive and exclusive hotel lobby. Would you be happy to be there? Would you feel like you belonged? Are you dressed appropriately? Would that matter to you? Would you feel embarrassed and try to leave or would you feel at home and immediately get a waiter's attention and ask for a gin and tonic?

Before you think about that scenario in too much depth, let's have a short quiz to pull out some of the values you hold that I think have relevance to interiors and interior design. As with other quizzes try not to think about your answers too deeply; try to answer quickly and instinctively.

Quiz time!

This quiz is designed to be illuminating and fun! Suspend judgement if you can and answer how you feel rather than how you think you should feel.

Instructions

Tick the values statement below that feel true for you.

Value statement	Agree or disagree
I deserve the best in home décor.	Agree/Disagree
I prefer to buy second hand than new furniture.	Agree/Disagree
I love luxurious surroundings.	Agree/Disagree
It's important that I feel safe at home. I have good security.	Agree/Disagree
I enjoy hosting friends at home.	Agree/Disagree
My home is for me and my family. We rarely invite visitors around.	Agree/Disagree
I care about the environmental impact of my life	Agree/Disagree
After an exhausting day, I am happy to get home and shut the door on the world.	Agree/Disagree
I want people to feel relaxed in my house.	Agree/Disagree
I am happy to mend and make do. I like an eclectic mix of interiors anyway.	Agree/Disagree
I love to express my personality through art on the walls and other objects.	Agree/Disagree
I aim to be well regarded by others and enjoy showing off what I have achieved.	Agree/Disagree
I love the sound of children's laughter in a home.	Agree/Disagree
My home is a place to retreat to and feel safe.	Agree/Disagree
I worked hard for my professional qualifications/ business achievements. I display my certificates and awards with pride, for others to admire.	Agree/Disagree
My home expresses my personality well.	Agree/Disagree

Did you spot the main values that I think have particular relevance to interiors in these questions? They are:

1   Environmentally conscientious. You love your eco credentials in the way you furnish and renovate your home. This might include finding old, vintage and preloved items, or renovating old items sensitively, or in the careful research you put into buying a new carpet or mattress. Your home is a mix of ecologically sound and thrifty buys. You may keep this to yourself (private) or love to show off your finds and ability to your friends (host).

2   Creative. You may be an artist, graphic designer, crafter, curator, fashion designer or anything else creative. Your home reflects your artistic style and tastes. You may keep this to yourself (private) or enjoy showcasing your creativity to many others (host).

3   Prestigious and powerful. You are status and achievement orientated. Your home is a reflection of your success and status. You may keep this to yourself (private) or love to show off your wealth and ability to your friends (host).

4   Private. Whatever your other traits, you are private. Your home is for you or for you and your family. You don't tend to invite people over. You put them off if they suggest it. Your home is a sanctuary, your place to retreat to.

5   Host. You are the host with the most. You love showing off your home and your style and approach to life. You put a lot of effort into people's comfort and happiness when they visit you.

6   Security orientated. For you, home is a safe place. An important refuge from the world at large.

7   Family oriented. For you, home is all about family, spending time with them, creating space in your home to facilitate family time.

You are likely to identify with one or more of these descriptions! For example, antiques are valuable and old. So you can be environmentally conscientious as well as being status oriented; or perhaps neither! Please add any notes about this to your overall picture PDF. At various points in this book I have pointed out the importance of suspending judgement. Our society is full of judgement and a sense of what is right and wrong. I would like you to forget about that for a moment. There is no more value in being creative compared to being rich. It all depends on your perspective. As long as you know and accept yourself, I think you will have a happier life!

Exercise

What have you learned from this exercise? Are there any surprises? What insights has it given you? Of the above values, which are most aligned for you? And do you feel that your personality IS expressed in your home? If not, are you starting to see how you might change things so that it is?

An opportunity for change

Please don't feel defensive about any of your answers. Whether you are a strident environmentalist or someone who likes the best of everything, your choices are yours and perfectly valid. If you uncover something you don't like then this might be the moment to decide that you are carrying an old belief, or someone else's viewpoint... and let it go. Some think that we can't change childhood memories or that beliefs and values are ingrained. This is not true. I believe that we can change anything if we want to. Sometimes it as simple as reviewing and deciding – becoming aware releases its power to influence, and in that moment you are free to decide what to believe in, as an adult.

Chapter summary

In this chapter we learned how our values affect the way we decorate our homes and the way we feel about our homes. And how this extends to how we feel about other people's homes and public spaces. Sometimes these feelings can be strong and at times we can feel quite self-righteous in our choices. in this book I guide you to suspend judgement of what is right and wrong, and instead focus on what will suit you personally in terms of your own home and what environments you choose to spend time in, when away from home.

A home for plants

Childhood experiences.
Family influences, and emotional memory

What can you remember from your early years? Most people's earliest memories are aged 3 or 4 years old, but they are fuzzy, unclea,r and possibly more of a result of family telling stories that are reinterpreted and recalled. Occasionally people have a clear recollections of their childhood, but most don't. Memory tends to be unreliable, so why bring it up? I'm including it because our early experiences are an important part of understanding our unique home interior preferences.

In early childhood when we are forming our personality we start to explore what we like and don't like, for example, most people dislike and avoid wearing the same colour as their school uniform. I ask clients about their early homes and their emotional reactions to the way those homes looked and felt. It is our reaction to our environmental experiences that are relevant here. I don't mind telling you that in writing this chapter, memories of childhood times at my grandma's house came flooding back. It was very emotional for me. She is now gone; her home was sold to another family a long time ago, but the feelings are still there inside me, attached to my memory of people and space. As a little girl of seven or eight, I was so excited to pack my little red case to go and stay with the affectionate, generous and wise lady who was an excellent cook and an even better hugger and player of games. And in my

A view showing the colour flow of reds and blues between the hall and the room beyond, by designer Emilie Heinonen

head, the dark room, warm fire, deep red rug, smells of cooking, nicotine-stained paintwork and sound of her singing in the kitchen are all very real and tangible in my memory.

My aim in this chapter is to raise your awareness of your early experiences and key emotional memories. The idea here is simple and twofold. If you can find the sweet spots from your childhood then you can replicate some of those good feelings today through features of your interiors that remind you of the past and rekindle those happy feelings. And, if appropriate,

you can avoid the things that bring back or evoke unhappy memories.

Unfortunately, some people do experience unhappiness in childhood and it is not my intention to add salt to a wound that you may have from your early years. The good news is that our past need not predict our future. As adults, we are in charge of what we think and what we choose to think. Building self-awareness around our preferences gives us control and choice. We have the power to decide and sometimes to change what we want and how we think.

Nostalgic memories

Below: holiday reading with views of Singapore harbour

If you feel you may need support while exploring old memories, why not complete the exercises in this chapter with a trusted friend?

Here's another personal example of what I mean. I was on holiday aged fifty, visiting my lovely friend Veronica, who lives in Singapore. One day I felt a little unwell, so

I stayed home to read a book whilst sitting on her balcony, which has amazing views. That day it was stormy and rainy. The balcony has a roof, so I was dry enough on the comfortable rattan-cushioned furniture. The rain came in tropical waves of intensity and the mist gently landed as spray on my face. It was warm fragrant rain and at one point I realised that I was feeling euphorically happy. It was a wonderful place to be, but if you remember, I was ill. The euphoria seemed way out of context to me. Not everyone sitting on that balcony would have felt the same. So, I wondered to myself, why was this experience so joyful for me?

Firstly, my scores on sensory dominance would be a clue. I am highly kinaesthetic. Which means I am very sensitive to atmosphere, temperature, humidity. I love an atmospheric storm. I can feel a change in atmospheric pressure and sometimes read clouds and predict the weather. But there was something else too. An early memory came to me. As a little girl, I loved to read adventure books. And, in the summer when it was raining but still warm, I had a favourite place to be when reading, which was in a fairly private doorway at home where you couldn't see me from the road. I used to open the door, lie on my tummy on the carpet, and read a book just out of reach of the rain. I loved the atmosphere created by the storm and the intimacy and privacy in my little space. I could feel tiny sprays of rain moisture on my face and breathe in the warm, humid and fragrant air.

Now, what might you design for me as a result of this revelation? A veranda? A front porch? A balcony overlooking a private garden? A summer house? Design is all about the identifying features and the details of this memory - near to rain but not getting wet, private, cosy, warm, scented, secret... Have I missed anything? What would you add in?

I want to help you to explore happy memories like this from your early years. The next set of questions are designed to help you access them. When you have some answers you can use them to evaluate your home and other environments that you spend a lot of time in. This part of the process is so individual, that the questions are longer than before and there are no multiple choices. It may help you, or be more fun to do this part in a conversation with a friend.

Childhood questions might be answered by old photo albums?

What are your environmental happy childhood memories?

- What's your earliest memory? Can you describe it? What is around you? Is there any significance to this that you can use today?

- Recall some of your happiest childhood memories. Where were you? Can you describe it? What is around you? Is there any significance to this that you can use today?

- How many times did you move in your childhood? Did this bother you? Which places were best? Why? What aspects of these homes come to mind?

- What style of house(s) did you grow up in? If there were more than one, which was the best and worst? Why? What aspects did you like or dislike? Have you repeated the positive features in your home now or do you have the opposite of something because you hated it as a child?

- How do you now feel about your childhood home on reflection? For example, was it spacious or small, warm or cold, formal or very relaxed? Were your parents house proud? Was your Mum fussy about anything? Did your Mum and/or Dad have hobbies? Were there any additional spaces like outbuildings, lofts garage or sheds? Were you allowed to have friends round to play, or did you go to other people's houses? What else can you recall? Sometimes we are clear about what we like because it is the opposite of the way we were raised.

- What other homes or spaces that have significance in your memory did you spend time in as a child? Describe your memories. Did a place stand out to you? Was there somewhere that you especially liked to visit? Why?

- Where did you spend your holidays? Describe the places. Where was your favourite? Was there anything about the environment that you especially appreciated?

- Did you have a childhood den or game? Describe it? How did you make it special?

- What hobbies did you enjoy, e.g. reading, modelling, painting? Was there anything about the spaces that you played in that you especially appreciated and might want to recreate? The light? The space? Any smells?

- Did you have a favourite place as a child in your home or garden or

The kinds of things we are looking for here are happinesses associated with a space, a character or person, colour or pattern, noise or sound, smell or taste, an atmosphere or touch. Or a combination of senses or other sensory memory, touch, noise, taste, and the space.

Some ideas that might help are: favourite foods, feeling cosy in a bedroom with a sloped ceiling, special birthday cake, always drinking out of a blue mug, a special plate design, rotating lamp shade, events that were special and particular items that were always present, reactions to clutter and cleanliness.

This is an area where some memories come to life when you talk to people who knew you then. Or sharing anecdotes with friends when their stories trigger your good memories.

Let me tell you a few client stories to help you access your own stories.

Imagine someone who is very neat and tidy with a strong habit of hygienic routines at home. She grew up in a home in the countryside with muddy floors and a family that were pretty lax around attitude to cleaning, tidiness and even food hygiene. Amazing for immune system building perhaps! All the way through her childhood she knew that as an adult she would live very differently. She now lives in an extremely clutter-free and clean home. She is not the kind of person who has objects on her countertop. Even the kettle and toaster have a place underneath the work surface. Materials are chosen for their glossy or shiny finish so that she can see how clean it all is. She clearly has rejected her early experiences and has a home absolutely opposite to the one she grew up in; from farmhouse to modern; from wood to acrylic; from rustic to shiny; from ramshackle and relaxed to formal and neat.

One client told me of his childhood growing up with two brothers in a small home without central heating. In the winter he had the choice of doing his homework in the warm noisy kitchen or

a cold quiet bedroom. Often he suffered the cold upstairs because he needed the quiet to be able to concentrate. He would sit in his coat, hat and gloves to do his homework and then return to the noisy family kitchen only after he had finished.

As an adult, having control of space, comfort and sound are especially important to him. He lives in a spacious, comfortable house now, but is consciously appreciative of it, and especially of personal space and acoustic privacy. The boy still exists within the man, many years later.

Some more ideas to help you to generate your own 'sweet spot':

- If you enjoyed den making and camping – why not have a canopy bed with draped softness.

- If you enjoyed reading and visiting libraries – perhaps install a well-stocked tall set of bookcase(s).

- If you lived overseas or in another part of the country – hang large landscapes of your favourite places and colour schemes that evoke the space.

- If you twirled happily in a 60s yellow leather iconic egg chair at your Grandparents – find furniture that swings and turns, or place pops of yellow items around your home.

Messy kitchen and (below) a sleek modern design

- If you made cakes and biscuits at home – design your kitchen with open shelves with well-labelled baking ingredients and some retro scales just like your mother.

The items can be large or small, expensive or affordable, portable, or architectural/structural. Let your imagination wander. Sometimes a trawl through a flea market or reclamation centre will trigger a happy memory. Other times a hotel or friend's home will remind you of something.

Of course if your recollections bring you unpleasant memories and associations, think about what features and spaces you might remove or avoid? You don't want environmental features that trigger any unpleasant memories and emotions in your home.

Psychologically fitting design

In his book 'Snoop', psychologist Sam Gosling describes his well-stocked and perfectly organised refrigerator. Sam confesses that he normally is low on the conscientiousness scale and yet his organised and full stocks of alcoholic beverages show unusually high conscientiousness behaviour traits.

He says, "I'll casually offer a drink and affect a calm demeanour, apparently unfazed that the ginger ale is now one bottle short; but as soon as the guest takes a bathroom break, I head straight to the storage cupboard and restore balance to my beverages".

Despite being a professional snooper and renowned psychologist, Gosling did not realise why he had this habit until he met a Texan architect called Chris Travis. Travis helps people identify their emotional and psychological associations as part of his architectural design process. He calls it 'psychologically fitting design'. Travis says that he will not design a home for someone until he has an in-depth understanding of their character. He helped Gosling to realise that, with his 'bottomless fridge' he was recreating happy summer days with generous grandparents who didn't restrict the desire that he and his brothers had for 'pop'. I'm fascinated by the idea that this architect wants to really understand his clients at a deep psychological level before he works with them. When Sam Gosling spoke to Travis's clients, he noticed something intriguing. Although they had gone through an in-depth approach leading up to the house design, after it was all finished they didn't have much awareness of what had gone into the thinking. They just knew that Travis 'got them' and perhaps, after you have gone through this book and made the changes you want to your home, you will do the same and the self-awareness you have built will start to fade. What do you think of that? Do you enjoy the self-awareness you are building or is it just a means to an end?

Exercise:

This is the final piece in the puzzle of your personality summary! How amazing! It's time to review your answers for this section for the last time.

- What features or spaces have you added, or could you add to your home that evoke happy memories from your childhood?

- What thoughts or ideas did the chapter or quiz raise?

- Write down all your thoughts on your summary.

Chapter summary

In this chapter we have looked at interiors from a unique perspective. The idea that bringing happy elements from childhood memories into your current home is a powerful one.

Our personality is formed early on in childhood and different types of surroundings have the potential to evoke happy memories as if they were safely stored there. It's worth spending some time to understand what objects and items and environments will evoke your happy childhood memories. Do this and you can create your own psychologically-fitting home design.

Chapter 14

A picture of your perfect space...

Pheeeew! That's quite a lot of information you've absorbed and worked through. Well done for getting to this point! I've taken you through all five aspects of personality: extroversion, openness, conscientiousness, agreeableness and neuroticism/ sensitivity; as well as mood preferences, values and beliefs, sensory preferences, colour choices, favourite styles and best childhood experiences! That's a lot!

The work you've done means you now have ALL of the ingredients to form a really comprehensive picture of your personality preferences for creating a home interior that's perfect for you! In this chapter I am going to take you through your notes step by step to make sure you distil all the answers.

You may feel that it's all formed neatly and makes sense already. Or you may be comfortable going through the information and prioritising what is important to you in an informal way. If that's the case, that's b r i l l i a n t, please do it your way.

Pulling it all together

However, I do understand that some of you may feel a bit overwhelmed and unsure of what

you've put together and what it means. For those souls, here's a guided process to help you make sense of what you've just done.

1. Read through all your notes. You've pulled out the key information from each chapter. Ask yourself "Is it complete?" If there are any parts you've missed or partially done, now is the time to go back and complete them.

2. Does it feel like a good summary of your personality, taste and preferences? If not, what's missing or what's wrong? This is a document for you and your use. Make any amends that feel right.

3. As you read through, more thoughts and insights may occur to you. Combinations of distinct parts of the book that make more sense, when put together. These are valuable 'aha' moments. They are golden nuggets of insight! Make sure you write them down! You may find you think about things away from this book. You might walk into a friend's house and see something that prompts a realisation. Make a note of it!

4. Stop. Prioritise and edit. This step is really important. Once you have done steps 1 to 3 you can narrow your notes and choices down. A lot of people's problems with making decisions in interiors is too much choice, which leads to feelings of overwhelm. It's important to decide which of these preferences mean the most to you? Find a way to highlight key words and draw lines between different elements that seem to connect with each other.

5. Finally, it is time to think about what that means for you and take action. Do you have a project in mind? Maybe you are really happy with how things are in your life and now you have insight into why that is. I expect though, that there are some small changes you can make straight away. To help you decide what to do, think about things like budget, timing, resources, and ease, and then pick off the easy things first. This will give you encouragement and confidence to tackle bigger jobs. Try not to take too many things on at once.

6. Have you done this quiz with a romantic partner or housemate and now you need to discuss your findings? If so, I've written the next chapter just for you.

7. For the longer term you might want to think about what your answers mean for ALL the spaces you spend a lot of time in - home, work and elsewhere. What is in your control to change and what isn't? For example, you may now have a heightened awareness of problems with your work-place. Can you request a solution? How might you go about that?

Your answers

	Area of personality		
Big Five	Highly open to experience, traditional, bit of both		
	Conscientious, easy-going, bit of both		
	Extrovert, introvert, bit of both		
	Agreeable, tough-minded, bit of both		
	Emotionally stable or more sensitive		
Preferred moods	Write down your 5 words		
Values	Write down your key values		
Sensory dominance	Visual		
	Auditory		
	Taste/Smell		
	Kinaesthetic		
Colour palette preference	Brights	Mids	Darks
Favourite colour combination			
Style preferences are			
Family memories	Evocative design elements to include		
Aha moments Further insights			

Actions/ideas:
What might you do now at home and work?
What are your short term and long term plans for improvement?

I am/prefer to be ...	Design ideas and thoughts

Pastel   Muddy   Neutral

Design elements to avoid

How my home shows my personality

Time for a real life example of the process and some images. Who do you think this country style, rustic, vintage and nature loving, boho, colourful and eclectic home owner is? That's right ha ha. Its me! My cottage looks like this.

I hope this example gives you a sense of how the elements of someones design personality come together in someone's home.

186

Chapter summary

In this chapter you have pulled all of your answers together to create a complete picture of your design personality. You now have a full explanation and guide to help you create spaces to suit you now and into the future.

But, if you live with your family or you are in a shared house with friends, you may be left with some questions about people who are different to you and how you might decide on design choices so that you are both happy with the outcome. Which leads us to the next chapter 'considering couples'.

My answers

	Area of personality
Big Five	Highly open to experience, traditional, bit of both
	Conscientious, easy-going, bit of both
	Extrovert, introvert, bit of both
	Agreeable, tough-minded, bit of both
	Emotionally stable or more sensitive
Preferred moods	Write down your 5 words
Values	Write down your key values
Sensory dominance	Visual
	Auditory
	Taste/Smell
	Kinaesthetic
Colour palette preference	Brights? No - too bright. Some mids and mostly muddy. Like Darks in moderation Pastel. Yes in moderation Neutral. Hate beige. Dislike most neutral spaces except white bedrooms.
Favourite colour combination	Dusky pink, coral, oranges, yellows, and blues. Bold or mid hue. Not primary – slight tint or shade. Energising. White bedroom – to relax Avoid green paint on walls but like plants.
Style preferences are	Rustic. Boho. Country. Modern. Not too fussy in details. No frills or bows. Natural materials. Wood, metal, eco paints. Wool, cotton, linen.
Family memories	Veranda from thunderstorm memory. Cosy nooks to read in. Back of shop. Cosy, Grandma's fire. Big garden for nature. Love nature & views.
Aha moments Further insights	Theme running through is love of nature and countryside, art and patterns have major nature influence. It's all about the 'feel' not the look. Need lots of creative stimulus. Tidiness shuts me down. I like being a host. The main things is people's relaxation and comfort. Quietness, nice scents creating deep relaxation.

Actions/ideas:
What might you do now at home and work?
What are your short term and long term plans for improvement?

I am/prefer to be ...	Design ideas and thoughts
Extremely high openness to experience	Love art and travel pictures. Busy patterns. Mix of patterns. Enjoy changing things around. Lots of stuff, books, art, ornaments.
Low. Conscientiousness. Easy-going. Untidy. High tolerance for mess.	Tidy up in blitz fashion. Like systems and good storage. Appreciate a cleaner.
Bit of both. Need time alone to recharge, love talking through ideas with others.	Like lots of warm colours and some darker and pastels but not neutral. Especially like pink and yellow combos.
Highly agreeable but also truth teller. Leads to inner conflict and sometimes conflict with others.	Home is comfy and easy. People say they can relax in my home, and I want them to. Need a comfier settee in lounge. Goal when redecorate.
Highly sensitive and also HSP. Some sentimentality.	Inspirational pictures, pictures of nature. Photos of loved ones. Beautiful art and objects. Lots of heirlooms especially china and glass. Making personal and unique items, e.g. lampshades.
Creative, joyful, relaxed, comfortable, energised.	Create comfy but energised and happy spaces. Full of chatter and music, food, and wine. Fun but in a relaxed way.
Down to earth, creative, honest, generous sociable/host, informal, environmental, mend and make do.	My home is your home. Not a show-off place. Come and relax and have fun. Mend and make do leads to creativity. And unique pieces. Highly individual space.
20	All senses are important, but K is by far the most important. How a place feels, quality of materials, textures, etc. Followed by noise. Really love peace and quiet.
25	
16	
39	

Clean lines, lack of clutter, shiny surfaces, fussy details, anything 'posh' or overly ostentatious.

Veranda space mix of indoor/outdoor. Create library room cosy nook. All books in one place and corner to read in. Find better way to organise ideas in offlce/studio. Currently great for creating ideas but need better help to bring them to fruition. Make my bedroom more serene. Add better storage. Log burner as focal point in lounge (not telly).

Chapter 15

Considering couples

So far we have looked at the world of personality and interiors from the perspective of an individual. You! It's a good place to start, but, of course, for most households, there's more than one person to consider. Although the number of single households in the UK and elsewhere is on the rise, couples, families and other types of multi-person households are more common (ONS: *Families and households in the UK*: 2019).

A couples perspective

People rarely discuss domestic home arrangements at the beginning of a romantic relationship, but perhaps they should? It could save a lot of arguments and tears later down the road. In their book 'Gifts Differing', Myers and Briggs discuss how differences in personality play out in relationships. There is an old saying that opposites attract, but, in research about long lasting relationships, this is debunked. Psychologists have found that the more a couple have in common, in personality terms, then the more likely they are to be with each other for the long term. Couples that are different in all personality traits have a much lower chance of long-term happiness. If you are in a relationship, you are probably like most couples; with some things in common and some areas differing. And I'm willing to bet that you are really aware of the areas of difference!

So, given this truth and the challenges many face, the question for many people then becomes, 'How do we create the perfect space when there is more than one personality to consider without creating a bland compromise or letting one person dominate too much?' Creating the home to suit the self becomes more complicated as the number of residents increases, but there are ways, and in this chapter I will share some hints and tips for couples to create a home that they both love and love to be in.

Occasionally a scenario I come across as a designer, is where one person in a couple thinks that they have 'taste' and dismisses the opinions and desires of their partner on that basis. As you know, I'm passionate about people creating homes to suit them, their personality and their mental and physical health and wellbeing. If one person doesn't feel 'at home' in their own home, then we are off to a bad start. For a moment, my role turns into that of marriage guidance or mediation.

So here's an appeal to anyone who shares a home and especially to couples! Respect your partner or housemate's difference in taste. My intention in this chapter is to offer you lots of information and tips to help you discuss your differences and then find a way to agree. If you change the 'I am right...' position and instead say 'I prefer...'; discussing likes and dislikes, wants and no-goes will feel much easier.

In the real world when I work with couples I do find more common ground than is at first apparent, so I hope you find that too. Most of the couples who consult with me, are people who really want to work together and agree on creating a home that they will both love to be in.

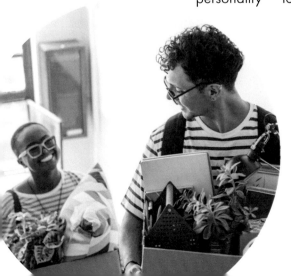

Process to follow

The first step, you won't be surprised to hear, is to do your individual picture on your own. As you are reading Chapter 15, you will hopefully not have skipped ahead, and you already have a fully completed individual design personality blueprint. Now it's time to ask your partner to do the process too. Let them work through the answers on their own. Do not confer at this point. That way you can be sure that each of your responses are truly yours.

When you have both completed your own picture then it is time to share. Here's a suggested couple's 'healthy discussion' guide for you. As well as a diagram for you both to use to make notes. You can photocopy the form in Chapter two of this book or go to my website for a link to a PDF version to print at home: www.lightandfrank.com

Take it steady

If at any point things get heated and frustrations boil over, perhaps leave the exercise and allow time for emotions to die down. I do understand that some decisions about home improvements are put off for many years so this conversation may at first bring up 'old' stuff. Try and persevere, using this method as your guide and take your time; it will be worth it in the end.

Many couples I work with have tended to focus in the past on where their tastes differ, or on points of conflict. This exercise can show up more areas of things they have in common, which is usually a pleasant surprise! I hope this is true for you too.

Let's look at the fictitious example of Barbara and John. They have been married for five years and live happily in a 3-bed house in the city. In terms of interiors and decorating, so far they have compromised a lot because they find it difficult to agree on what they like. They are frustrated with their safely neutrally decorated home and want to make it more of a reflection of them and their personalities.

Your design personality discussion: guide for couples

What do you have in common?

a   Start with what you have in common. Where are you the same in personality terms and where do you agree on things you like?

b   Write those aspects in the middle where the circles overlap.

c   Discuss these areas in depth.

d   Also talk about where you agree on what you both don't like. It can be very helpful to agree on what you both really dislike. That's a whole load of options 'off the table'!

e   Are there any surprises in what you've found out? Note them down.

Where are you different?

a   Move on to where you are different and write those aspects in each of your individual circles. Take your time to discuss your likes and explain what you like and why you like it.

b   Some of these areas will be where one or both of you holds strong opinions and there will be other areas where you and your partner are prepared to be more flexible. It's really worth noting down both of these areas for each element. You may be able to bargain for something you love but if your partner isn't keen they get to do the same elsewhere. If you love something and your partner hates it then that is going to be difficult. Perhaps though, you love something and your partner is indifferent. That means that they can put up with it because they know it gives you a lot of happiness? And hopefully vice versa.

• Does the overview explain the root cause and areas where you find it difficult to agree on things?

• Finally, how might you use this information to help you design and decorate your home in the future?

• What can you take action on as a result of this conversation?

Barbara

Extrovert
Agreeable
Visual and kinaesthtic
Comfy
Relaxed
Likes Parties
Childhood at the
beach. Enjoying
camping and
caravanning outdoors
Flexibly uses spaces
Mainly bright colours
Some pastels

**Light and
airy spaces
Textures &
tactile surfaces
Clean lines
Conscientious
No clutter
Black and
white**

John

Introvert
Sensitive
Auditory
Thoughtful
Quiet
Traditional
Friendly
Industrial
City childhood
Enjoys large
abstract art
Mids and neutrals
Own private chair

The key areas for negotiation for Barbara and John will be:

- How colourful and busy the spaces will be as Barbara is higher on extroversion. They both like high contrast, and black and white schemes so maybe adding a few small pops of colour would please both of them?

- How sociable each of the spaces in the house will be. It may be that they decide to create two dedicated spaces: a sociable area or room for Barbara to entertain friends as well as a quiet place for John to spend restorative time alone. Then they could decorate each of the spaces more in line with their own preference, rather than a compromise.

- What else do you think Barbara and John will talk about?

So now it's your turn.

- What will you talk about?

- Where do you usually get stuck and has that now changed?

- Where are you similar and where are you different?

On the following pages I am sharing my tips for navigating differences by the Big Five personality traits and other aspects of individual difference.

Design tips for couples who differ on the introvert - extrovert scale

Do you remember that this trait is all about energy and how you manage your need for interest, excitement, stimulation and restoration? You will have a different 'score', but it is rare that someone with very high extroversion and very high introversion will be romantically involved because their preferred lifestyles will be so different? Although you will feel different, it's unlikely to be in the extreme. One way to consider differences in this and other personality traits is to think of your scores on a continuum. Someone who is very extroverted may feel like most other people are introverted because in relation to them, they are.

Just like colour, with personality, it's all relative. Most people are not at either of the extreme ends of the scale of introversion and extroversion; many lie somewhere in the middle. Sometimes this is called ambiversion.

Here are some suggestions for couples where there is some difference on the introversion/extroversion trait:

- Discussions and decision making. If you are more extroverted than your partner it will probably be in your nature to dominate and appear more confident with your opinions.

Remember that your opinions are not better because you are more confident (or expressive). Both of your preferences and opinions are equally valid. I encourage those of you that are more introverted to confidently stand up for what you prefer. This may take time and practice if you haven't done it much so far. I encourage you both to take the time because once you have decided and spent money and time redecorating, any decisions you have made will be visually apparent for you both for many years to come! Changes after the event, because one person really can't live with i,t can be time consuming and costly. Has this happened to you?

- Compromises. A home with too many compromises on colour, pattern and style choices, will end up being too bland and boring and you will feel that it reflects neither of you. Instead of compromising in a 'toning it all down way' use the Venn diagram and talk about which ideas each of you are passionate about and which you might feel more easy going. There will be some colours or items you hate, some you can tolerate, some where you don't have strong feelings either way and, some things you love. Take the 'I hate it' options off the table and work on the rest. Try and ensure there is give and take on both sides, not just one side.

- Zones. One way to get more of your own way is to create zones. Review the roles and time spent in certain areas of your home and allow more say where there is more ownership. For example, if one person cooks more, and spends a lot of time in the kitchen, you might decide that it's fair to let that person have more say in the kitchen design layout, materials choices, and style and colour schemes. Conversely, in areas where you both spend equal amounts of time, more care can be taken to include both person's needs. And don't forget the garden. It becomes another room or series of rooms to use in the summer. You may be lucky enough to have a summer house/outdoor office to include in your evaluation of zones.

- Bedrooms. If you have a large enough home, bedrooms are just used for resting, sleeping, dressing and intimacy, not working, gaming, socialising, etc. The dominant mood scape for a bedroom is usually calm, so in this room I would advise that the more introverted person gets a bit more say because it's a lot harder to dial down our response to stimulus once encountered. Sorry extroverts! One work-around that you may agree to is to create a dynamic feature wall behind the bed head, or using the bed head. This is stimulating and interesting and you see it when you are getting changed and are spending time in your bedroom, but is not as visible when you are lying in bed.

- Hallways and downstairs loos. These are spaces that you either pass through or spend less time in. Extroverts you could persuade your partner to agree to more adventurous design here, perhaps, and then you can visit the space when you need a stimulus boost!

- Views. Consider who has what view and decorate in a bold and subtle way incorporating both preferences. For example, if two of you share an office, you can create a view to look at that the other person has their back to. In this way, each person has the view they like in the room, and that view will help them work to their best.

- Home Office. Many people work from home at least some of the time. In order to be stimulated, especially if they work alone, extroverts will need things to look at, background music and items on display. Whereas introverts will enjoy working alone and prefer a calmer quieter and simpler environment. In this scenario, using storage where things can be easily taken out and hidden away at the end of the workday will be helpful for all.

- Multipurpose spaces If you are space limited and have multipurpose rooms in all areas including the bedroom, e.g. you have a desk in the corner then think carefully about zones and views so that you can switch off mentally and relax. Room screens and hidden storage are useful tools to hide clutter and work activity.

A colourful and busy space. In this lounge space we have a mix of stimulus in colour style and texture. Pale surfaces are brought to life by texture coloured and textured throws and cushions a vibrant green sideboard. This is the kind of scheme that might suit a couple who differ on the personality trait of extroversion

Design tips for couples who differ on the openness to experience scale

Those high on openness have an active imagination, enjoy variety and trying new things. Those low in openness prefer more traditional décor, routine over variety and stick to what they know. Those higher in openness that like change will want more change in the home and have a higher desire to redecorate and to do so more often. Too much change is stressful for someone lower in openness. As I write this I can almost hear conversations up and down the country, "I've had another idea for the kitchen" is met with a groan," But we only redid it 4 years ago. It's fine as it is. Isn't it?"

Here are some suggestions for couples where there is some difference in this trait:

- Desire to decorate. The desire for change can be met in many ways, e.g. new job, new car, new clothes, change of holiday destination, etc. To meet both of the couples needs the higher openness person may meet their need for change in multiple ways so that the person who has higher need for stability and sameness at home will achieve it, for at least some of the time, in some of the space. There are many ways to satisfy high openness to experience needs beyond the house.

- Smaller changes. This suggestion also meets environmental concerns. Move things around rather than replace them. For example, you may have a gallery wall or objects of interest on shelves. A change around and redistribution of art and loved items will help you see them again. This is a straightforward way to create a feeling of change to satisfy people who have a desire for more change in the home.

- Clusters. Display items like photos and art in certain parts of the house in clusters rather than dotted about everywhere. This means there are some relatively free areas for the lower openness scorer to view and relax, whilst still retaining areas where the high openness person has an outlet for their creative or adventurous pursuits. Even the most stimulation seeking personality needs a space to 'visually' rest their eyes sometimes.

- Zones. In the same ways that I suggested above, allow the person who uses an area of the house a lot on their own more say about what happens in that space.

A collection of old tin boxes and containers. These objects of interests can evoke joy in the heart of one person and yet mystify another who see it as old rubbish or trash.

Tips for couples who differ on the conscientiousness scale

One thing I notice about people high on conscientiousness is that they tend to think that their view of the world is correct. It's not! You may feel strongly about this, but you are not right just because you like things to be tidy. The current trend for de-cluttered minimalist spaces is just a preference, not an ideal to aspire to, despite what the supporters of it say.

What's more important (than proving who is right) is that you agree a standard that you can both commit to. This is such a potentially emotive area. People with higher conscientiousness scores can love to occupy the high moral ground here. And I'm not letting the messier types off the hook here either. The aim is for you to agree how to create a home that suits you both and does not create excess stress for one or both of you in achieving it.

Here are some suggestions for couples where there is significant difference in this trait:

- Agree on a rota of chores that is fair and shared. Decide which you prefer and which you hate and divvy it up fairly. Then stick to it!

- If you can afford it, employ a cleaner to avoid rows. A good cleaner will help you keep up standards and eliminate any discussions about who created the mess

- Agree on having some messier areas/dumping grounds for the messy ones to use on a daily basis and agree a time scales (e.g. once a week) when they need to be regularly cleared up, so they don't overflow or get out of hand.

- Talk about the little things that wind you up, e.g. cups dumped in the sink, how to load the dishwasher, laundry routines, etc.

- Allow a mixture of some planned activities and some freedom for spontaneity in the home, because if you remember, this trait is about levels of planning and spontaneity as well as cleaning and following rules and general tidiness.

- Agree times for clearing out excess stuff like old clothes and dispose of items to recycling centres and charity shops where possible.

- And finally, if you don't want to get rid of it, but don't want to see it, get better storage to hide it all!

Effective storage is often a good solution for couples that are different on the personality traits of conscientiousness and also introversion and extroversion. In particular glass fronted cabinets can please both personality types. This is because the items are on view which means they can be seen and this acts as stimulus for extraverts. However, the glass front reduces dust and germs which pleases the person with high conscientiousness. Of course items need to be kept tidy and the glass needs to be cleaned regularly so there is still plenty to negotiate here.

Tips for couples who differ on the agreeableness scale

If you have differences on the agreeableness scale then the things you debate may not seem to be about interior design at first. You may debate things like furniture layout, temperature, and the amount of effort to put into hosting others when they visit you in your home. Or even if people are allowed to visit at all!

The main tip here is to understand each other's views and preferences. The agreeable person will be really uncomfortable if they are restricted from hosting the way they like to. The less agreeable person will find this difficult to understand. This will show up in discussions about drinks, food, music choices, how much decorating and preparations are necessary.

You get the picture. It's basically anything that links to people's comfort and enjoyment in relation to your home.

And some of the time, it might be fair to give the less agreeable person a rest and let someone else be the host; or see friends and family elsewhere, in other settings and keep your home just for you.

Tips for couples who differ on the neuroticism/ sensitivity scale

Of all the Big Five traits, neuroticism or sensitivity is the one where there is a known statistical difference between the scores of men and women. Women are more likely to score higher than men. So, in a normative heterosexual male - female pairing the discussion about interiors preferences might heat up in this area where the woman wants more sentimental objects and objects of comfort in the home and the man does not understand their purpose. Of course every couple has their take on this. Some men are very sensitive. Some women less so.

The main tip here is to, yet again, put effort into understanding each other's position and preferences. The sensitive person will need items in the home that help them to feel safe and secure. They will want to keep sentimental items and will be more sensitive to temperature, smell, and sound than their more emotionally stable partner.

Affirmation sign

For the less sensitive person in the relationship, try to be empathetic to your partners needs even if you don't understand them. As stated earlier you may see sentimental objects as unnecessary because you have no need of them. Try to remember this is just your perspective, it is not fact. There is no such state as 'too sensitive' or 'too insensitive'. Some people are more sensitive and some people are less sensitive. When you take a perspective where all opinions and tastes are valid, harmony follows. And hopefully decisions and agreement too.

Tips for couples who differ on their sensory dominance

As there are five different senses this section could be quite long, and a lot has already been covered in Chapter 9. Needless to say by now, the key thing for couples is to learn about and understand your partner's sensory dominance and your own and then negotiate how you can accommodate each person's priority areas in various parts of your home.

Here's a few ideas you might find useful:

- For couples that differ on visual sense dominance, some things to consider and discuss include: what is the right level of visual stimulus for each of you, paying particular attention to colour family preferences, colour saturation levels, patterns and colour combinations, as well as lighting levels and material choices. The person with higher dominance in the visual sense will want colour choice accuracy. Your partner will probably not understand or see the importance of getting exactly the right colour or why you care so much about buying quality paints and wallpapers. I've created a longer section on colour on the next page.

- For couples that differ on the auditory sense dominance, some things to consider and discuss include: sound management and electrical equipment; getting the balance of soft and hard surfaces in the space correct; budgeting for investing in quality sound systems for music, gaming, TV and also quieter domestic appliances. These things will cost more but will be important for the person who has auditory dominance.

- For couples that differ on the olfactory gustatory sense some things to consider include: being considerate with chemicals for cleaning and minimising the use of things with strong smells, artificial scents and bleach. It might be nice to investigate VOCs when you are buying new stuff. It's worth investing in good ventilation and fans to bring fresh air into the house.

- For couples that differ on the kinaesthetic sense some considerations may include: being considerate about the feel of materials and understanding that this is sometimes more important than how they look. Also allow investment in high quality or unusual materials, or more kinaesthetic items like throws, rugs and carpets.

Tips for couples who differ on colour choices

It may not be a specific colour that you end up arguing about. It may be that because of differences in the need for environmental stimulus, it is the vibrancy of colours or the combination of colours that you find hard to agree on. If this is the case, here are some questions to help you get to the bottom of that:

- Which of the colour families do you prefer? For example, brights, darks, neutrals, etc.

- Do you like contrasting colours like the complementary scheme? Or similar ones like in the harmonious schemes?

- Do you prefer high contrast or low contrast colour schemes? A high contrast theme would be something like black and white, low contrast something like whites and creams.

- Collect colour charts and create piles of favourites to see what you have in common as a couple. Separate colours into piles of colour combinations you really like, quite like, can tolerate, and really don't like at all.

Mood boards can really help here because some people find it much harder to visualise what someone else is describing. If you want to persuade your partner to be more courageous with colour schemes, create a mood board of all your ideas and show them how they can work together. Or take them to an example of what you want in a café or a friend's house where there is a similar colour scheme so they can see what it looks like.

Tips for couples who differ on their styles

Style differences can go quite deep into our family stories and personality needs. As with everything else though, go through all the styles that you really like, quite like, could tolerate if you had to, and absolutely despise, so on no account would agree to. If you have been at deadlock in the past I think you might be pleasantly surprised that you find some areas of agreement. Couples who disagree on their interiors tastes tend to focus on what they disagree on, so, when they follow my process, they are pleased that there is something they have in common. There are loads of styles that you can choose from, so I'm confident that you will be able to find some common ground. And some of the agreements will be about what you both dislike, which is almost as helpful as what you like, because, as stated before, fewer options are now 'on the table'.

A quick note on families and shared living

I could write so much on families but have to slow down somewhere. So, for purposes of this book, I have just written a few tips to help resolve family disputes based on personality differences.

The scale of challenge you are faced with will depend on the size of your home and family. And this will change as your family grows. In a similar way, if you live in a shared house, the scale of your challenge will be linked to the size of the house, how many people you share with, and how different you are from each other.

As with couples, start with asking everyone in the family or home to do the quizzes and then get together to talk about how similar and different you all are in your personality and taste preferences. Here are some thoughts and questions to get you talking.

Questions to help get you talking:

- Whose opinion and preferences dominate? Is that fair? Discuss this and decide what is more fair and inclusive. Do you need to rebalance things a bit?

- If your children are fortunate enough to have their own bedroom, then that is a space where they can express their personality and create a sanctuary from the world. Talk to them about how they might do this and how you might help. Budgets and managing expectations are key here. Also, beware of fads. You don't want to redecorate bedrooms every couple of years so pick key times with your children so that they enjoy the space for a few years at least. All children develop at different rates, so I haven't suggested ideal ages for redecorating.

- If you have a family room or all spend a lot of time in one space in the house you may decide to all have an input into how it is arranged and decorated. In a shared house the rooms you will probably want to discuss together are the living room and the kitchen.

- Shared houses are usually owned by someone else, so some of your choices may be limited by rules such as no paint colour change, no more holes in the wall to hang pictures etc. You may also be restricted by budget. Try not to let this put you off. Much can be done to improve space on small budgets and on items that can be removed and taken with you when you move on. I have seen some great examples of temporary wallpaper, wall vinyls, and tile stickers, and of course furniture, lighting and accessories are all easily changeable.

- You may be a very inclusive family and wish to allow your children to have a say in the décor of the whole house. Great! Do go ahead. But I think it's also ok to let the parents dominate choices in the shared space. After all, when children grow up and move home they will have the chance to express their personalities in their own homes.

Chapter summary

If you use my approach in your discussions you will be able to go further into understanding what space design(s) will suit your relationship or family as well as yourself. If you have been in disagreement about decorating decisions in the past, this process will hopefully help you to unlock some of the issues.

The key to agreeing and deciding, is listening carefully to each other's preferences, respecting differences, finding common ground, as well as ways to both agree and disagree and making allowances for each other along the way.

This personality process may bring many differences to light. Look for what you have in common to help you make decisions and try to only be insistent on the things you really care about. Here are some examples of when it is probably best to just let it go:

- If someone loves their aspirational posters and you think they are naff, hold your tongue?

- If someone really takes ages setting up a sound system that you think sounds just the same as the other one, perhaps there is no need to say so?

Above all, love, respect, tolerance and understanding will lead to a harmonious and happier home. We all want different things. How lovely, when we can find a way to have them.

I wish you lots of luck and patience in your discussions!

Chapter 16

Next steps

People approach their interior makeovers in a wide variety of ways. Some like to do a little bit at a time and others jump in with very extensive plans for change. Before you start, there are lots to consider: budgets, timetables, availability of trades to help, time of year (for jobs that entail exposure to the elements) and of course how much disruption you can cope with.

Although makeover shows usually change everything in sight, most people don't have the budget or desire for a clean sweep, so current objects that are staying, need to be considered and accommodated. And, of course, if you are at all sensitive in your personality, or nostalgic, the idea of getting rid of everything is the last thing you want to do.

Before I talk about inspiration and planning, there's something I want to make reference to: the 'red thread'.

The red thread theory

Throughout the book I've talked about design from the context of individual room schemes but what if you have a few rooms or a whole house to do? Some designers subscribe to the red or golden thread idea. So let's briefly discuss what that means and whether it will or won't work for you.

The red thread theory is an idea where instead of individual room designs a concept design is created for the whole home. This creates a flow through the home of same or similar colours, materials, lighting, furniture style, flooring and textures. Like many design principles it is often described as something that people 'should' do. Of course, you know me by now, so you won't be surprised to know that I don't think a lot of that exhortation.

The red thread is a good idea if you're the kind of person who likes things to match or feel uniform, so the personality types of low openness to experience and high conscientiousness are likely to approve. And often I see neutral homes decorated with similar colour palettes and materials in each spaces so this is probably favoured by introverts rather than extroverts.

However, this approach is probably not for you if you are high in the openness to experience trait and like quirkiness and variety in your home. Let the individuality of each space be your 'red thread' instead!

Inspiration

The first thing you need, in order to get started, is to find some inspiration. Luckily, inspiration is everywhere! And you needn't limit yourself to pictures of interiors or fabrics and colours. You might be inspired by a scene in a film, beautiful art, the latest fashion, weather, the sea, a visit to a museum, city scapes, gardens and flowers, book illustrations, old photographs, a walk in the woods, the soft fur of an animal, and materials like glass, old stone and wool; even a dream can be inspiring. Whatever you find needs to conjure up the mood that you are looking for.

It's a good approach to collect your ideas as they come to you, either in note form or in an app like Pinterest. The important part is that you have them all in one space, so that you can later evaluate what you have and start to create a room scheme.

Pinterest is a popular space for collecting images on virtual boards. If you use it, my advice is to try not to fill your board with too many images. If you do, then create an

extra refined one for each space. The first board is everything you find. The second is much more limited to the things you really like and think will go together well. Less confusing! Once you have a curated selection of images, you can start to put together a mood board.

What is a mood board?

Throughout this book I have talked about mood boards, but you might be wondering what a mood board is and what the difference is between a mood board, a concept board and a sample board? In interiors the words are often used interchangeably but there are differences. So here's a quick explanation.

A mood board is a visual collection of items which aim to convey feelings and ideas and this may have actual images of furniture and samples too. A concept board also aims to conjure feelings but is more purist and shouldn't contain any pictures of interiors at all. A concept board is used as the starting point of the creative process, with images that stimulate and inspire. Finally, a sample board is literally one full of samples: paint chips, tiles, wallpaper, flooring and pictures of furniture and fittings. The sample board is the last and essential step when checking material and paint quality and colours. In larger commercial projects, separating out these processes is helpful, but you may wish to merge one or more in your planning. So when I use the term mood board in this book I'm really including all three processes.

Mood boards by Holly Wicks, designer/maker (left) and Emilie Heinonen, designer (right)

Putting together your physical mood board

Place together chosen items for your interior on a physical or virtual area. It's an effective way to collect inspirational ideas, materials, colours and pictures of furniture and fittings as well as check choices and colours. You can get a sense of proportion and scale here too. Review your budget as you make your choices. My tip here is to apply your budget in a way that means you spend money where you will notice it the most.

Once you have your mood board and have started to select fixtures and fittings, you need a plan.

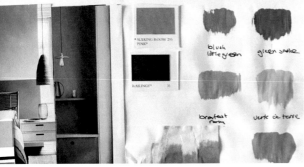

A good plan includes a detailed list of what needs to be done, and very importantly in what order. If you stick to this flow of what to do in what order, I promise you that you won't go far wrong. Here is a guide to planning for a successful home makeover.

Essential planning:

1. Overall goals: What are you hoping to achieve and by when? What's your budget, rough plan and who needs to be involved in any decisions? Scope it all out.

2. Restrictions: What restrictions do you have? Budget? Grade listing? Conservation area? Do you need to consider planning permission or building regulations?

3. Function: What's the main function/ purpose of room/space. Is it multipurpose? Who uses it the most?

4. Feelings: How do you (and others) want to feel in the space? E.g. a kitchen might be energised, happy, sociable, and creative; a lounge might be calm and relaxed.

5. Layout, Space & FFE: Consider how you plan to use the space (to meet function and feeling needs) and where you will place furniture and fixtures. Does it need to be flexible or is it going to be fixed? Check measurements and ensure that the scale of furniture chosen is proportionate to your space. Make sure there is

room to move easily around the furniture. Consider electrics and lighting for that layout (and other layouts if you want flexibility).

6   Design Process & Planning: Plan it all before you start. Think about all the materials, paints, fabrics, fixtures, and furniture you will need and where you will source them (link to budget). Lay out for real on a sample board so you can see all your choices together. I recommend ordering samples, especially paint, and materials like fabric and floorings. Colours and textures on a screen are not the same. And don't forget the small details like light switches and decorative moulding and woodwork.

7   Edit/decide: Get more than you need and then edit it down to create your final design!

8   Trades: Do you plan to bring in trades, DIY, or a bit of both? What needs to happen in what order? If you have completely drawn up a plan of works, i.e. any electrical and plumbing work should be done first and decorative finishes and flooring

last. Don't be too optimistic in your planning. Build in contingency time as things often shift. Find trades people you trust by asking for recommendations from friends and testimonials from a trusted trades person you already know.

9   Budgeting: Allow contingency in your budget too. At least 10%. Ideally more. This is especially important on bigger jobs. Something unexpected nearly always crops up.

10 Keep calm: Patience, persistence, and a calm attitude is what you will need once you start. Things will go wrong! Understand that trades people often have to juggle jobs. Sometimes things crop up, so it's hard to estimate how long things will take on your jobs and other jobs they may be committed to.

11 Stick to the plan: Don't be a magpie! Decide on what you want and stick to the plan. Deviating during the process may mess up your design, disrupt the timetable, annoy trades and blow your budget. If you need to, spend more time planning, and don't rush the start.

Final thoughts

I truly hope you enjoyed this process of discovery and you are now looking at yourself and your home with a new perspective.

We have covered many aspects of what makes you unique to enable you to build this picture. Let's look at them again: openness, conscientiousness, extroversion, agreeableness, neuroticism/sensitivity, mood, sensory dominance, forms and styles, colours, values and family background. This is quite an extensive list but there is always more to explore in the understanding of the human mind and our personal preferences.

By now you will have a good understanding of how complex determining personality and taste preferences really is. This is not a simple quiz that will give you a quick answer. It is a rich and involved process that will give you as much as you put into it.

I really hope you found this process insightful, useful and fun.

Wishing you happy and harmonious living!

Love and light

Michelle xx

Notes, resources and further reading

Aron Elaine, *The Highly Sensitive Person* Harper Collins

Augustin Sally, *Place Advantage* John Wiley & Sons

Barralet Adam et al, *Gifts of the Essential Oils* Alchemy House

Berne Eric, *Games People Play* Penguin Random House

Bernheimer, Lily, *The Shaping of Us* Robinson

British Psychological Society, www.bps.org.uk

Cain, Susan, *Quiet*, Penguin Random House

Cattell, Raymond, *The Scientific Analysis of Personality* Taylor & Francis

Cobb, Matthew, *Smell: A Very Short Introduction* Oxford University Press

Danish Institute of Happiness, www.happinessresearchinstitute.com

De Sausmaurez, Jane, *Basic Colour. A practical handbook*, Herbert Press Ltd

Eiseman Leatrice, *The Complete Color Harmony: Pantone edition*, Rockport Publishers Ltd

Finlay, Victoria, *Colour. Travels Through The Paintbox*, Sceptre Press

Gosling, Sam, *Snoop* Profile Books

Haller, Karen, *The Little Book of Colour* Penguin Random House

Jones, Russell, *Sense* Wellbeck

Kassia St Clair, *The Secret Lives of Colour,* John Murray

Kopec, Dan, *Environmental Psychology for Design* Bloomsberg

Laborde, Genie, *Influencing with Integrity*, Crown House Publishing

Lidwell, William (video series), *How Colors Affect You: What Science Reveals* from The Great Courses

Myers, Isabel Briggs and Briggs, Peter, *Gifts Differing, Understanding Personality Type*, Davies-Black Publishing

MacLeod, June, *Colour Psychology Today* O Books

Steele Valerie, *Pink! The history of a punk, pretty, powerful colour*, Thames & Hudson

Steg, L. et al, *Environmental Psychology: An Introduction*, Wiley & Son

Wright, Angela, *The Beginners Guide to Colour Psychology*, Colour Affects Ltd

Dedications

This is my first book and I could not have written it alone.

I am deeply grateful to Sarah Cook for pushing me to develop my ideas and share them in the first place. Also to Jos Steinmann for reminding me that I was going to write a book about the process that he had been through.

Thank so much to my beta readers who have given me brilliant feedback along the way; some harsh but necessary, for example I thank Gary Nemorin for the request for simplified quizzes and my sister Becca Armitage for the encouragement to include more examples. Also many thanks to Frances Butt for pointing out that I had used the word neurotic and neurotism way too often for most people's tastes!

Many other lovely friends gave me amazing feedback on the writing and other aspects of the book including book cover ideas. Grateful thanks to Victoria Anderson, Leisa Foxlow, Becky Barnes, Julie Moore, Emilie Heinonen, Cathy Vass, Paul Higgins, Tris Steinmann, Kirsty Northover, Bex Stanton and Jenny Shaw.

In a professional capacity I thank Amy Morse and Lottie Storey for great author coaching and marketing support, Nicki Mors for the photo permission work and Kath Hooper for my author bio (it's almost impossible to write your own!). And of course Berenice Howard Smith, book designer, for making my ideas look beautiful on the page.

I've had so much encouragement from friends and family, often meet ups would start with an inevitable question "How's the book going?" Sigh! It's a tricky one to answer sometimes.... Well, now I have the answer. Here it is and in 3 different versions; print, ebook and audio.

Many thanks to the lovely designers and home owners who gave me permission to use their images to explain a personality perference or show a design style. Each of you are generous, amazing and so talented.

And finally the most heartfelt thanks go to my friend Helen Blenkinsop, who has been a enormously helpful and constant source of writing advice, knowledge and support. I simply could not have written this book without her help.

About the author

Michelle Armitage is not your run-of-the-mill design consultant. She recognises that design tastes are as varied as personalities. What's beautiful to one person is clutter to the next.

Michelle's approach is to uncover the preferences, traits and quirks of her clients before she designs a space to make their soul happy.

Never one for a prescriptive path, Michelle's multifarious career has taken her through several job roles, locations and interests, always learning more about what makes people tick. From HR consultancy to interior design, her knack for creating a safe and vibrant space for people has been constant.

In her personal life she loves spending time in nature, enjoying wide open spaces and expansive skies. Whenever possible she loves to travel and explore different cultures, architecture, art and people. At home she's often found rummaging for treasure in flea markets and vintage stores.

Photo Credits